MOVIE STARS

UNSEEN ARCHIVES

Gareth Thomas

Photographs by the
Daily Mail

p

This is a Parragon Publishing Book
This edition published in 2005

Parragon Publishing
Queen Street House
4 Queen Street
Bath, BA1 IHE, UK

Photographs © Associated Newspapers Archive
(additional photographs by Getty Images - see page 318)
Text © Parragon 2005

Produced by Atlantic Publishing Ltd
Origination by Croxons PrePress

ISBN 1-40546-743-6

Printed in China

Introduction
From Actors to Movie Stars

Florence Lawrence can lay claim to being the first movie star. Working for the Biograph studio in the pioneering days of the film industry, Lawrence was hugely popular—though fans knew her simply as 'The Biograph Girl'. When a rival company poached her from Biograph, her new employers hyped up their prize acquisition by sensationally revealing her identity. For the first time, fans of 'the flickers' could put a name to an actor.

All the studios soon followed suit, trumpeting their own acting wares and reaping the rewards at the box office. Movie actors were suddenly movie stars.

Florence Lawrence didn't enjoy the limelight for long. Her career fizzled out, and she was supplanted by the likes of Chaplin, Pickford, Fairbanks and Valentino, who became the first true screen legends.

Using stunning pictures from the *Daily Mail* archives, many reproduced here for the first time, *Movie Stars Unseen Archives* features a stellar cast of acting greats, from the stars of the silent era to those taking the honors at the 2005 Oscars.

MOVIE
STARS

UNSEEN ARCHIVES

THE KING OF COMEDY

From humble beginnings in London's music halls as a youth, Charlie Chaplin was to rise to stardom as probably the greatest comedic actor of his day, and is still acknowledged as one of the kings of comedy. Having traveled to the US in 1912, he joined Mack Sennett's newly formed Keystone company in 1913, which quickly became renowned for its hectic slapstick movies. Chaplin was an able pantomimist, but was soon to bring something more to his pictures. By concentrating on developing the personalities of his characters, notably that of the Little Tramp, his best known and oft revisited creation, Chaplin brought a humanity and humility hitherto unseen in slapstick, and set himself apart as an actor with genuine talent and artistic integrity. He also quickly proved himself to be a capable director, and although the pace of his output slowed from 1916 to 1936, with total artistic control, Chaplin made perhaps his greatest works. Many of Chaplin's later and rather less successful movies were somewhat darker in mood, perhaps reflecting the off-screen tribulations that he endured during the McCarthy era, as he faced the threat of both personal and political scandal. However, in 1972, just five years before his death, Chaplin was awarded a special Oscar for his 'incalculable' contribution to movie-making.

Left: Charlie Chaplin addressing a huge crowd of fans in 1921.

A WOMAN APART

Amongst the most enigmatic and beautiful of Hollywood actresses, Greta Garbo began her career in her native Sweden before arriving in America in the 1920s, where she appeared in a number of silent movies before making her first 'talkie', *Anna Christie*, in 1930. Whilst many actors failed to make the transition, Garbo continued to enchant audiences with her ability, whilst her beauty added to her allure. She also tended to shun publicity, famously declaring 'I want to be alone', which was seen by many as part of her mystique; however, some instead came to regard her as whimsical and aloof. She withdrew from the limelight completely after 1941's *Two-Faced Woman*, and despite later offers and negotiations, she was never to work in Hollywood again.

Left: Garbo in her second American picture, *The Temptress*.

Right: In an early silent movie, *Flesh and the Devil*.

'OUR GRACIE'

Above: Gracie Fields (second from the left) with her understudies in the *The Show's the Thing*. A singer before turning her hand to acting in 1931, Lancashire-born Fields quickly became a star of stage and screen in England, whilst also selling numerous records. Hollywood was somewhat more hesitant, fearing that her humor and style were too peculiarly British, but she was offered a four-movie deal in 1938, which saw her become the world's highest-paid actress.

A STIFF UPPER LIP

Right: John Mills was first brought to the attention of the public in the 1930s by Nöel Coward, who cast him in a number of productions after having seen him as a repertory actor in Singapore. Although he was to appear in a variety of roles throughout his long career, Mills was probably best loved and will be best remembered for his numerous war movies of the 1940s and '50s, in which he invariably played a stiff-upper-lipped British officer, and although he was to receive an Oscar for Best Supporting Actor in *Ryan's Daughter* (1970), it was perhaps his quintessential Britishness that precluded greater Hollywood success.

HOLLYWOOD'S GOLDEN COUPLE

Above: Although she played some serious roles, Carole Lombard was best known as a comic actress, having learned her trade in the 1920s working with Mack Sennett, founder of Keystone studios, and the man that gave Charlie Chaplin his first big breaks. After being paired with Clark Gable in *No Man of Her Own* (1933), in which the couple were wed, an off-screen romance developed, and Lombard and Gable married in 1939, becoming known as Hollywood's golden couple. Tragically, however, Lombard was to die in a plane crash in 1942, leaving Gable broken-hearted.

Opposite: Charlie Chaplin in *Modern Times.*

CULT FOLLOWING

Above: W C Fields in *Mrs Wiggs of the Cabbage Patch* with ZaSu Pitts. A successful vaudeville performer, in the 1920s Fields made a few silent shorts, but it was during the 1930s, with sound, that his comedy came into its own. Fields typically played pompous, misogynistic and cynical characters, supposedly not far removed from his own, which, whilst not to everyone's taste, earned him a large cult following. After a long fight against illness and alcoholism, Fields died on Christmas Day, 1946.

Opposite above: Fred Astaire with his wife Phyllis Potter in 1937.

Opposite below: Astaire and Ginger Rogers in *Roberta*. Following an early screen test, one casting director noted that Astaire could 'dance a little'. It was to prove a massive understatement as Astaire went on to achieve legendary status for his dancing prowess in numerous musicals, notably in partnership with Rogers, throughout the 1930s.

IT HAPPENED ONE NIGHT

Opposite: Claudette Colbert in a scene from the 1934 Frank Capra classic romantic comedy *It Happened One Night*. Colbert was to win Best Actress award for her role but, apparently unconvinced of her chances, she failed to attend the ceremony.

Left: An unconventional beauty perhaps, but Bette Davis was to receive ten Oscar nominations during her career, and win two Best Actress awards. The first came in 1938 for her performance in *Jezebel*, after which she was nominated in five consecutive years.

Below: Bob Hope pictured in 1939 with Margaret Lockwood, the year after she starred in Hitchcock's brilliantly dramatic and humorous *The Lady Vanishes*. Whilst Lockwood was to become hugely popular in Britain during the 1940s, Hope was to attain even greater acclaim in the US.

IN THE FLESH

Left: Laurence Olivier in a stage production of *Hamlet* in 1937, having recently starred in a movie version of *As You Like It*. Olivier was to perform in numerous Shakespeare productions on both stage and screen, and as his movie profile grew, he attracted countless fans to the theater who were eager to see him in the flesh. Regarded by many as one of the greatest actors of all time, he received ten Oscar nominations during his long career, winning just one for *Hamlet* in 1948.

Opposite: Gracie Fields in a scene from the 1939 comedy *Shipyard Sally*.

LEADING LADIES OF THE 1940s

Above: Olivia de Havilland in the 1946 thriller *Dark Mirror* in which she played identical twins, Ruth and Terry Collins. That same year she would receive the Best Actress award for her part in *To Each His Own*, and three years later achieve the same accolade for *The Heiress*.

Opposite: Veronica Lake, at the time of filming the western *Ramrod* (1947). For many she was the classic '40s vamp.

A NATIONAL INSTITUTION

Bob Hope enjoyed a long and varied career, making his name in radio before becoming popular as a stand-up comedian and a star of both the silver screen and television. Although born in England, he came to be regarded as a national institution in the US, even entertaining at the White House. In the movies he is probably best remembered for his series of 'Road' movies, starring alongside Bing Crosby and Dorothy Lamour.

Left: Hope with his wife Dolores Reade at a Royal Command Film Performance in London's Leicester Square.

Opposite above: Entertaining troops in 1949.

Opposite below: Mobbed by autograph hunters.

THE LOST WEEKEND

Left: Welsh-born Reginald Truscott-Jones changed his name to Ray Milland early in his acting career, which no doubt made it easier for him to secure parts. He gave his finest performance in 1945, playing an alcoholic in *The Lost Weekend*, which earned him the Oscar for Best Actor that year, whilst the movie received Best Picture, and Billy Wilder was awarded the Oscar for Best Director.

Opposite: Elizabeth Taylor in 1947, aged 16. Taylor began her career as a child actress in such movies as *Lassie Come Home* (1943) and *National Velvet* (1945), but it would be some years before she would achieve true stardom.

Below: John Mills with his wife and Lord Courtauld-Thomson, attending a Royal Command Performance in 1948.

'COOP'

Opposite: Gary Cooper in *The Fountainhead* (1949). In a career spanning five decades, Cooper, affectionately known as 'Coop', was a consistent box-office draw, and regarded as one of the greats, particularly amongst his peers. He was rewarded with two Best Actor awards, for *Sergeant York* in 1941 and *High Noon* in 1952.

Right: Gene Kelly pictured with his wife Betsy. Along with Fred Astaire, Kelly was one the most important of Hollywood's musical talents, directing, choreographing and starring in numerous movies during a long and distinguished career. He is probably best remembered for his dance sequence to the title song in *Singin' in the Rain* (1952).

Above: David Niven and his wife Hjordis leaving a London register office after marrying in 1948.

BONNIE PRINCE CHARLIE

Opposite: Upon his arrival in Hollywood, Scottish-born David Niven was assigned a code number and a note describing him as a stock English actor. Although he became somewhat stereotyped as an English gent, and the material that he was offered was often second-rate, he played his parts with such charm that he was to enjoy a long and successful career. In 1948 he was able to revisit his roots, playing the lead in *Bonnie Prince Charlie*.

Left: Joan Fontaine in 1949. Fontaine followed her older sister Olivia de Havilland into the movies, and was the first of the two to win an Oscar, taking Best Actress for her performance in 1941's *Suspicion*.

Below: Despite questionable acting ability, and a sometimes scandalous off-screen life, Lana Turner, also known as 'The Sweater Girl', had huge sex appeal, and was able to found a long career upon it. Her best performance was probably as a femme fatale in the classic thriller *The Postman Always Rings Twice* (1946).

MRS OLIVIER

Above: Vivien Leigh backstage in 1950 after a performance of *A Streetcar Named Desire*. Leigh played the role of Blanche, and is pictured with her French counterpart Arlette Bathiat, or 'Arletty'. The following year, Leigh was to play the same part in the screen version of the play, for which she would receive her second Best Actress Oscar, the first coming after perhaps her most famous role, as Scarlett O'Hara in *Gone with the Wind*, which also claimed Best Picture and Best Director in 1939. In 1940 Leigh married Laurence Olivier, and although they were to play a couple in only one movie, *That Hamilton Woman*, they were frequently to be found on stage together.

Opposite: Discovered by Howard Hughes in 1941 and cast for his movie *The Outlaw*, much of Jane Russell's early career was beset by controversy concerning the promotion of her rather obvious 'assets'. Indeed, *The Outlaw* was itself outlawed for some time, and later movies would also be subjected to censorship. However, she was not without ability, proving to be a hit alongside Marilyn Monroe in *Gentlemen Prefer Blondes* (1953).

AN ENDURING LEGEND

Opposite: Gloria Swanson became a star of silent movies during the 1920s, working with such directors as Mack Sennett and Cecil B DeMille. However, her career took a downturn in 1928 after the collapse of *Queen Kelly*, in which she had personally invested a fortune. It would take until 1950 and the success of *Sunset Boulevard* for her to recover both financially and artistically. She is pictured that same year with daughter Michelle.

Left: Elizabeth and Robert Taylor (no relation). A fixture at MGM for 24 years, Robert Taylor equaled Clark Gable's record for remaining with one company.

Below: British star Trevor Howard with his wife. Despite never winning an Oscar, Howard was well regarded as an actor on both sides of the Atlantic, and is perhaps best remembered for his performance in *Brief Encounter*.

OLD BLUE EYES

Opposite: Frank Sinatra at a children's charity event in London in 1951, which he had conceived of at an earlier meeting with the Duke of Edinburgh. The Duke had asked him to help the cause because of the similar work he had done for children across America. Sinatra became a show-business legend as a singer, actor, producer, and tycoon, and although his career went through a brief lull in the early '50s, in 1953 he was to win an Oscar for Best Suppporting Actor in *From Here To Eternity*.

Below: Comedic actor Danny Kaye with Wilfred Pickles and the George Mitchell Choir at the Festival Variety Show in 1951. Born in Brooklyn in 1923 as Daniel Kaminsky, Kaye began his career early, performing on stage while still at school.

Left: Joan Fontaine en route to make a radio broadcast in Paris.

LEADING LADIES

Opposite: Born Jeanette Helen Morrison, Janet Leigh was discovered whilst still a young music student, chang-ing her name as she embarked upon a career in acting. Her most famous moment in a movie, and probably that of director Alfred Hitchcock, was her slaughter in the notorious 'shower scene' in *Psycho* (1960). However, it has been suggested that the scene was directed not by Hitchcock, but by Saul Bass.

Above left: Tasmanian-born Merle Oberon outside her London hotel, dressed for the Ascot Gold Cup in 1950. She is probably best remembered for her role as Cathy in a 1939 version of *Wuthering Heights* opposite Laurence Olivier, although ironically it was not one of her better performances.

Above right: In 1949, Claudette Colbert lost out on appearing in *All About Eve* after breaking her back. However, the following year she was to make a successful recovery and star in the harrowing *Three Came Home*.

BOGIE AND BACALL

Above and opposite: Humphrey Bogart and Lauren Bacall in 1951. The couple met on the set of Bacall's first movie,
To Have and Have Not in 1944, married the following year and went on to make *The Big Sleep* (1946), *Dark Passage* (1947) and
Key Largo (1948) together. Both had a natural affinity for playing tough, cynical, somewhat defensive characters, and it was often
said of Bogart that he was always playing Bogart whether on or off screen. Either way, there was a clear chemistry between them;
their collaborations were effective and their relationship successful.

TEARS OF A CLOWN

Opposite: Buster Keaton arrives in England with his wife and his trademark mournful expression soon after his appearance in *Sunset Boulevard* (1950), a movie he later claimed never to have seen.

Right: Katharine Hepburn arriving in London clutching a hat, a sack, a lute-like instrument, and a bow and arrow. She was returning from the Congo, where she had been filming *The African Queen* with Humphrey Bogart.

Above: Audrey Hepburn attending the premiere of *Pool of London* in 1950. Prior to the movie being shown, Earl Mountbatten presented the British Film Academy awards. Drawing comparisons with her namesake Katharine, she took Hollywood by storm in the 1950s.

NOTHING TO DECLARE

Above: Elizabeth Taylor shows off her new transparent purse and its contents in 1951. She made the journey from the US to England to work on the big-budget, medieval swashbuckler *Ivanhoe*, which also starred Robert Taylor and Joan Fontaine.

Opposite: Taylor attending a performance of *Kiss Me Kate* at the London Coliseum in 1951, the year that she received acclaim for *A Place in the Sun*. However, she was perhaps most successful during the 1960s.

NEVER LET ME GO

Below: Clark Gable during the filming of *Never Let Me Go* (1953). Ironically, MGM had decided that they would not be renewing his contract after completion of the picture.

Opposite: Zsa Zsa Gabor married George Sanders in 1949. Sanders had made his money in textiles and tobacco before turning his hand to acting. The couple worked together on *Death of a Scoundrel* in 1956, but by 1970 they had divorced, and Sanders married her sister, Magda.

Left: Joan Fontaine in 1952, the year that *Something to Live For* was released. Although she continued to work into the 1970s, for many this movie was one of her last good works.

WORK AND PLAY

Above: Italian actresses (from left to right), Lila Amanda, Cosetta Greco and Gina Lollobrigida at Victoria Station in London, having arrived for an Italian festival at the New Gallery Cinema.

Opposite: Aside from show business, golf was a major passion for Bob Hope. Here he can be seen playing in an Anglo-American charity match alongside Bing Crosby, against stars of British radio, Donald Peers and Ted Ray. Apart from having a shared interest in golf, Hope and Crosby worked together often, in the 'Road' series of movies.

HIRED GUNS

Above: Alan Ladd with a group of extras during the filming of *The Red Beret* in 1952. He had begun his own career as an extra, before his big breakthrough, *This Gun for Hire* in 1942 with Veronica Lake, with whom he would go on to make *The Glass Key* (1942) and *The Blue Dahlia* (1946). Despite being diminutive in stature, Ladd tended to play the role of the tough guy, perhaps most memorably in 1953's *Shane*.

Opposite: Ladd being attended to by technical advisor Major E T Russell on the set of *The Red Beret*.

PAT AND MIKE

Below: Katharine Hepburn with Robert Helpmann (centre) and Cyril Ritchard during rehearsals for a stage production of Bernard Shaw's *The Millionairess* in 1952. A movie version starring Peter Sellers and Sophia Loren was to be released in 1960.

Left: Regarded as one of the greatest actors of all time, Spencer Tracy had a long relationship with Katharine Hepburn, first starring with her in *Woman of the Year* in 1942. Here, he is pictured some ten years later, when they worked together on *Pat and Mike*.

Opposite: Douglas Fairbanks Jr and his wife outside their home in 1952, following a break-in which resulted in the theft of jewelry worth almost £2,000. Fairbanks Jr was the first example of the second generation of a family to become a movie star, but he never quite achieved the greatness attributed to his father.

LEADING MEN

Opposite: Richard Burton in 1952. Burton was born in 1925 in South Wales, the twelfth of thirteen children, and began acting at an early age, traveling to London at 16 before gaining a scholarship at Oxford. He moved from the stage into movies in the early 1950s, receiving his first acclaim in 1952 for *My Cousin Rachel*, in which he played opposite Olivia de Havilland.

Above: Trevor Howard leaving a party at the Savoy Hotel, London, with Helen Cherry, Joan Greenwood and Peggy Cummins. He would later be arrested and charged for driving under the influence, fined £50 and banned from driving for a year.

Right: Humphrey Bogart and Lauren Bacall aboard a cruise liner arriving in Plymouth, England. Their first child, Stephen, was born in 1949, and Bacall was soon to be expecting a second.

DOUGLAS IN GREAT DEMAND

Opposite: Kirk Douglas with Brigitte Bardot. A university wrestling champion who turned professional to put himself through drama school, Douglas's first big movie success came with *Champion* (1949), in which he played a boxer. He was suddenly in great demand and took on a number of roles, many portraying brooding, obsessive, self-destructive characters. Off screen he was said to be aggressive and egotistical, but his tenacity enabled him to found his own production company, Bryna, in 1955.

Above: Gregory Peck (right) visiting Alan Ladd and Joan Tetzel on the set of *Hell Below Zero*, shortly after Ladd's huge success in *Shane* (1953). Peck was also highly successful by this time, having received an Oscar nomination for his first big role, as Father Chisholm in *The Keys of the Kingdom* in 1945 and nominations the following two years.

THE NICEST MAN IN HOLLYWOOD

Above: At the peak of his career, Gregory Peck, dubbed by some as the nicest man in Hollywood, traveled to Britain to make two movies for Rank, *The Million Pound Note* (released in the US as *Man with a Million*) and *The Purple Plain*. Here he is pictured shopping for suits for *The Million Pound Note* in London's Savile Row, 1953.

Opposite: Peck with his nine-year-old son Jonathan arriving at London Airport from Paris. Having filmed *Roman Holiday*, which earned co-star Audrey Hepburn an Oscar, Peck spent the next 18 months in Europe.

STUNNING BEAUTY

Above: Ava Gardner dressed in lace, fur and diamonds arriving at the premiere of Alan Ladd's *The Red Beret* in 1953. A stunning beauty, she could also act, which she proved that same year playing opposite Gregory Peck in *The Snows of Kilimanjaro*.

Opposite: Audrey Hepburn sporting extravagant three-tiered earrings at a premiere in 1953. From relative obscurity in London's West End, to fame on Broadway in *Gigi*, Hepburn was then catapulted to stardom by an Oscar-winning performance in *Roman Holiday* opposite Gregory Peck, all in the space of two years.

FRANK AND AVA

Above: Frank Sinatra greeted by his wife Ava Gardner upon his arrival in London from New York for a European tour. Following on from her success in *The Snows of Kilimanjaro*, Gardner was to appear in *Mogambo* with Clark Gable in 1953, earning her the only Oscar nomination of her career and third place in a *Box Office Magazine* poll.

Opposite: Olivia de Havilland with her three-year-old son, Benjamin. Although she had decided to concentrate on stage performances in the early 1950s, she appeared in *My Cousin Rachel* opposite Richard Burton in 1952, with some success.

LA LOLLO

Opposite: Italian actress and cover girl Gina Lollobrigida, known as La Lollo, examining a sequined dress as she searches for outfits for a new movie. Already something of a star in her home country, she received wider attention after appearing opposite Humphrey Bogart in *Beat the Devil* (1953) and *Trapeze* (1956). Her greatest successes were in Europe, but after resolving contractural problems she made a series of movies in America during the 1960s.

Right: Vivien Leigh, resplendent in diamonds, attending the premiere of the comedy-drama *Escapade* in 1955, at which time she had returned to the stage with husband Laurence Olivier.

BEST ACTRESS

Opposite: Greer Garson preparing for a BBC broadcast in London in advance of a tour of British universities lecturing on Shakespeare and film. From 1941 to 1945 she was nominated for an Oscar every year, winning Best Actress for *Mrs Miniver*, and she was to receive a further two nominations during her career.

Left: Born in Berlin in 1901, Marlene Dietrich rose to Hollywood stardom during the early 1930s, appearing as a glamorous vamp in a series of Josef Von Sternberg pictures. Her movie career slowed somewhat after the two parted company, but in the 1950s she revived her fortunes with an international cabaret career.

Below: Marlon Brando with Sophia Loren in 1954, the year he won his first Oscar for *On the Waterfront*.

THE BAREFOOT CONTESSA

Opposite: Ava Gardner in 1954 at the height of her popularity, she was once described as the most beautiful woman in the world.

Left: Ava Gardner returning to the US from Spain having completed filming on *The Barefoot Contessa* (1954), the story of a Spanish gypsy dancer.

Above: A 28-year-old Richard Burton being presented with the traditional Hamlet Medal by the Mayor of Elsinore, Denmark, after playing the lead in a production of *Hamlet* at the town's annual festival in 1954.

HEPBURN'S TWELVE NOMINATIONS

Left: Having performed in *The Millionairess* on stage in both London and New York, Katharine Hepburn returned to England in 1954 with a view to making a movie version with director Preston Sturges. Backing for the project eventually fell through however, leaving her available for *Summertime* (released as *Summer Madness* in Britain), for which she received another of her eventual twelve Oscar nominations.

Opposite: Following the success of *Roman Holiday*, Paramount attempted to buy Audrey Hepburn's contract from Associated British, but it made more sense financially for them to lease her to them. She was to make her second movie, *Sabrina*, in 1954, starring with Humphrey Bogart and William Holden.

LOREN IS ITALY'S FINEST

Opposite: Rising star Sophia Loren, voted Italy's most popular actress, prepares to attend the opening of an Italian film festival in London, 1954.

Above: Mr and Mrs David Niven, Mrs Stephen Mitchell and Kenneth More during an interval at the premiere of *After the Ball*, which featured Laurence Harvey, best known for his role in *Room at the Top* (1958).

Left: The ever-extravagant Zsa Zsa Gabor flew into London in a converted bomber belonging to Porfirio Rubirosa, dressed in mink and pearls, before taking a taxi to Claridge's.

GENTLEMEN PREFER BLONDES

Left: Jane Russell in 1954, the year after her success in *Gentlemen Prefer Blondes* with Marilyn Monroe, and a year in which she would again become the subject of controversy, much as she had following her debut, *The Outlaw*, in 1943. The movie this time was the lighthearted musical, *The French Line*, and the censors objected to certain camera angles, and a costume that appeared to be struggling to contain her at times.

Opposite: From around 1955 onwards, Katharine Hepburn dedicated less of her time to acting in order to devote more time to Spencer Tracy, whose health was rapidly deteriorating. However, they would work together one last time, in *Guess Who's Coming to Dinner* (1967), for which Hepburn would receive another Oscar.

REBEL WITHOUT A CAUSE

Right: Born in 1931, James Dean began acting at school and went on to secure minor parts in three movies in 1951 and 1952, before gaining some work in television and theater. It was whilst on stage that he was spotted by Elia Kazan, director of *A Streetcar Named Desire*, and cast in the role of Cal in *East of Eden* (1955). He continued the theme of teenage angst in *Rebel Without a Cause*, which also featured a young Dennis Hopper, before demonstrating his range in *Giant*. Only days after he had completed shooting, he crashed his Porsche and was killed. Despite his short career, his tragic and untimely death, together with his good looks and on-screen intensity have assured him a place as an icon.

Opposite: Richard Burton in rehearsals for Shakespeare's *Henry V* at the Old Vic Theatre, London, 1955. Well regarded as a stage actor, it is often said of Burton that he failed to live up to his potential on screen.

NEWLY-WED AUDREY

Opposite: Newly-wed Audrey Hepburn arriving at Los Angeles Airport in 1955, to begin filming *War and Peace*, in which she would co-star with her husband Mel Ferrer. Hepburn was to play the role of Natasha, with Ferrer as Prince Andrei. Director King Vidor revealed that Hepburn was the only actress considered for the part.

Above: Janet Leigh of *Psycho* fame in 1955, the year that she made *Safari*. In a career of more than fifty movies, Leigh worked alongside many of the great stars of the time including James Stewart, Gary Cooper and Judy Garland.

THE MAN WHO KNEW TOO MUCH

Above: James Stewart with Doris Day, who starred together in Alfred Hitchcock's re-working of *The Man Who Knew Too Much* in 1956, 22 years after he had directed the original. It was Stewart's third collaboration with Hitchcock, following *Rope* (1948) and *Rear Window* (1954).

Opposite: Stewart seeing his wife off at London Airport as she returned to Hollywood to be with their children. Stewart, however, remained behind to complete work on his latest movie.

KELLY'S INVITATION TO THE DANCE

Opposite: Gene Kelly in 1955. Work on *Invitation to the Dance* had begun some two years earlier, but it would not be released until 1956. When questioned over rumors that it was too revolutionary for release, Kelly assured the press that it was both revolutionary and would be distributed. Much of the delay was owing to the fact that a section of the movie was to be in cartoon form, but this would eventually be released separately.

Left: Janet Leigh on her way to Paris to spend time with her husband Tony Curtis. Two years previously they had appeared together in the biopic *Houdini*.

Below: David Niven, Ava Gardner and Stewart Granger on their way to Rome, for filming of *The Little Hut*. In 1956, Gardner and Granger also starred together in *Bhowani Junction*, whilst Niven played Phileas Fogg in *Around the World in 80 Days*. The movie featured cameo appearances from a huge number of stars, including Noel Coward, Marlene Dietrich, John Gielgud, Buster Keaton and Frank Sinatra.

DOUGLAS FAIRBANKS JR

Above: Douglas Fairbanks Jr and Colette Wilde in *The Last Knife*, one of a series of TV productions made after his last full-length movie in 1951. Fairbanks Jr had no great passion for acting, regarding himself as an imitator rather than a creator; however, he had a famous name, good looks and a wonderful voice.

Opposite: Gary Cooper in *Friendly Persuasion*, a lighthearted, somewhat sentimental Civil War western, based on a novel by Jessamyn West. It went on to win a Grand Prix at Cannes.

STEIGER'S HEAT OF THE NIGHT

Opposite: Rod Steiger takes a call from a friend whilst relaxing in his hotel room. Steiger began his career in television, making his movie breakthrough with *On The Waterfront* in 1954, which earned him an Oscar nomination. He went on to become a prolific and sometimes great actor, with noted performances in *The Harder They Fall* (1956), *The Pawnbroker* (1965), *Dr Zhivago* (1966) and *In the Heat of the Night*, for which he won the 1967 Oscar for Best Actor.

Left: Vivien Leigh attending a premiere during the 1950s. Although she had returned mainly to theater productions after bouts of ill health, she gave a good performance in *The Deep Blue Sea* (1956).

SHAKESPEAREAN ACTOR

Opposite: Richard Burton in another Shakespearean role, or in fact roles, for he and John Neville were to alternate the parts of Othello and Iago in a production of *Othello* at the Old Vic, London.

Right: Sophia Loren attending a film festival in Tivoli, Italy in 1956, the year before she would make her first Hollywood movies, *The Pride and the Passion*, with Frank Sinatra and Cary Grant, and *Boy on a Dolphin*, with Alan Ladd.

INDISCREET

Ingrid Bergman with friend and favorite
co-star Cary Grant at a costume test for
the film *Indiscreet* in 1957, which was
based upon the Broadway comedy *Kind
Sir*. Bergman arrived in Hollywood from
Sweden in 1939 and became the top
female star during the 1940s, featuring in
such movies as *Casablanca* (1942) and
Gaslight (1944), for which she received
the first of her three Oscars. She caused a
scandal in the early '50s by having an
affair and a child with director Roberto
Rossellini (whom she would later marry),
and for a time was ostracized by
Hollywood, but by 1956 all had been
forgiven and she was to win Best Actress
for the title role in *Anastasia*.

HITCHCOCK'S FAVORITE

Cary Grant was born Archie Leach in 1904 in Bristol, England and first travelled to the US in 1920 with a touring company. By 1932 he had secured his first Hollywood movie and within three years had risen to stardom. He acted in several comedies throughout his career, but he was also one of Alfred Hitchcock's favorite leading men, appearing in the thrillers *Suspicion* (1941), *Notorious* (1946) with Ingrid Bergman, and *North by Northwest* (1959).

Left: Grant arrives in London to begin filming *Indiscreet* with Ingrid Bergman. It was produced at the famous Elstree Studios, but a number of scenes were shot on location in and around London.

Below: Grant and Bergman chat to PC Sidney Goodwin, who is on duty during shooting in Golden Lane, London.

Opposite: Grant and Bergman on location at London's Royal Opera House, with members of the Royal Ballet, Margaret Lee and Brenda Bolton.

AN AMERICAN LEGEND

Opposite: John Wayne on his way back to the US, having completed filming on *Legend of the Lost* in Africa with Sophia Loren in 1957. Wayne made his name as a tough guy in a succession of Westerns, the best of which were directed by John Ford. His rugged, overtly macho character lent itself well to such roles, and for many Wayne encapsulated something of the spirit of the pioneers who conquered the American West.

Left: Tony Curtis with one-year-old daughter Kelly in 1957. Not usually seen sporting a beard, he was growing it for *The Vikings*, in which he would appear with Kirk Douglas.

Below: Curtis and Ernest Borgnine, studying the projector at a special Technorama showing in London.

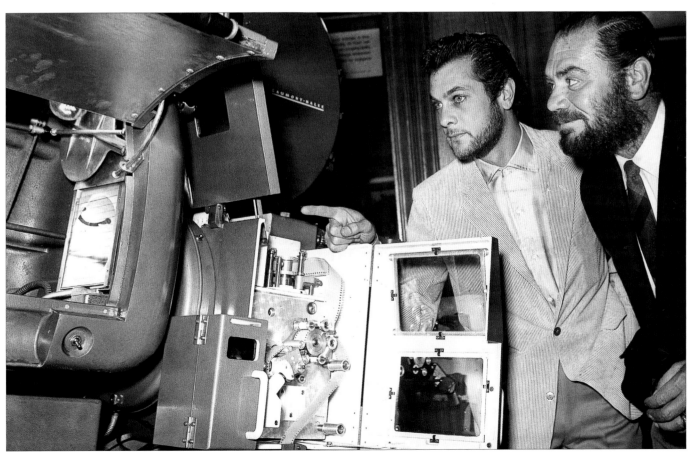

DENCH'S OPHELIA

Opposite: A young Judi Dench in 1957, rehearsing the part of Ophelia in *Hamlet* at the Old Vic, at the beginning of a long and distinguished stage career. Her first appearance in a movie came in 1964, and although better known for her work in theater and television, she has made a number of appearances in pictures and won an Oscar in 1998 for her portrayal of Elizabeth I in *Shakespeare in Love*. She was made a Dame in 1988, the year she also began to direct plays.

Right: Lana Turner filming *Another Time, Another Place*, in 1957. The following year a scandal would erupt when her lover, gangster Johnny Stompanato, was stabbed to death by her 14-year-old daughter. However, her career was undamaged by the event and was perhaps even boosted by notoriety.

ACTRESS FOR HIRE

Above: Bette Davis taking a country walk in Berkshire, England, in 1958. With a lack of offers for parts, Davis placed adverts in the movie press around this time, and work was soon forthcoming.

Opposite above: Frank Sinatra and Lauren Bacall in 1957, the same year that her husband Humphrey Bogart died.

Opposite below: Tony Curtis with Kirk Douglas and his wife. Curtis and Douglas were appearing together in *The Vikings*, which Douglas's company was also producing.

ITALIAN GLAMOR

Opposite and left: By 1957 Italian actress Gina Lollobrigida's Hollywood career had begun to take off but, pregnant for much of the year, her next appearance was to come in 1958's *Anna of Brooklyn*. In 1956 she had been replaced by Sophia Loren in the last of the '*Bread and Love*' series, and later, Loren would also take her part in 1965's *Lady L*, after the project had originally been abandoned some years earlier. This no doubt contributed to a lasting rivalry between them, as Loren began to challenge La Lollo's position as *the* Italian glamor girl.

WILLIAM HOLDEN'S 10 PERCENT

Above: William Holden in 1957, the year he was to appear in the hugely successful classic, *The Bridge on the River Kwai*, which was to take that year's Oscar for Best Picture. His contract for the movie ensured him 10 percent of the gross, effectively assuring him a substantial annual income for the rest of his life.

Opposite: Holden in London after five months of filming *The Bridge on the River Kwai* in Ceylon.

THE NEW BRANDO AND BERGMAN

Above: Paul Newman and his actress wife Joanne Woodward in 1958. Newman was being hailed as
Brando's successor, whilst Woodward was referred to as a 'home-grown Bergman'. The couple had
met during the filming of *The Long Hot Summer*, and were married soon afterwards.

Opposite: Kirk Douglas and his wife attempt to avoid the British weather, sheltering from the rain
beneath his coat. There is no question of avoiding the photographers who have gathered to take
their picture as they arrive from Los Angeles, but they seem happy to oblige.

FONDA AT HIS BEST

Left: Between 1948 and 1955, Henry Fonda left Hollywood and returned to Broadway, coming back to star in *Mister Roberts* directed by John Ford, with whom he reportedly came to blows during filming. He went on to make *Twelve Angry Men* in 1957, which whilst not a huge box-office hit, earned him critical acclaim. Fonda himself reckoned it to be his best work.

Opposite: The band plays on while James Cagney and Cara Williams take a break during the filming of *Never Steal Anything Small* (1958).

Below: Swashbuckling legend and off-screen Lothario Errol Flynn dining with actress Beverly Aadland, having completed filming of *The Roots of Heaven* in Africa.

PROUD REBEL

Opposite: Olivia de Havilland, in 1958. Now living in Paris with her French journalist husband, Pierre Galante, de Havilland professed that her interest in movies had waned. However, she was to give an excellent performance that year in *Proud Rebel* with Alan Ladd.

Left: Charlton Heston with his wife, attending the premiere of the epic *Ben-Hur*, a typically heroic role for the actor, and at the time, the most expensive picture ever made, at a cost of around $15 million.

Below: Sir Alec Guinness with Yvonne Mitchell, Valerie Hobson and Janette Scott at a luncheon held in his honor in 1959, two years after winning Best Actor for the role of Colonel Nicholson in *The Bridge on the River Kwai*. He was knighted the same year.

ROCK HUDSON WEDS

Opposite: Rock Hudson with his wife Phyllis Gates. Gates was the secretary of Hudson's agent, and it came as some surprise to his fans when it was revealed that Hollywood's number one bachelor had married in secret at the Santa Barbara Biltmore Hotel.

Right: Clark Gable in monogrammed smoking jacket, shortly before making his last picture, *The Misfits* (1961), with Marilyn Monroe, which was also to prove her last completed work.

Above: Gina Lollobrigida attending the premiere of her latest picture, the biblical epic *Solomon and Sheba*, which starred Yul Brynner.

GANGSTER NUMBER ONE

Opposite: Edward G Robinson became Hollywood's number one on-screen gangster after demanding, and getting, the lead role of Rico in *Little Caesar* in 1930. He is seen here almost thirty years later, on his way to a Moscow premiere.

Above: An unusually domesticated-looking Errol Flynn with his third wife Patricia. Flynn was rakish to the end, however, becoming involved in an affair with Beverly Aadland with whom he worked on his final project, *Cuban Rebel Girls* in 1959. A year later, he would be dead from a heart attack.

Left: 'Sex-kitten' Brigitte Bardot demonstrating her characteristic pout.

WAYNE'S BATTLE FOR THE ALAMO

Opposite: John Wayne attending the premiere of *The Alamo*, which he produced, directed and acted in. Released in 1960, he had been working on the project for some 14 years, and at great personal expense.

Above: Musical great Gene Kelly shares a smile with actress Donna Anderson at a reception following a showing of *Inherit the Wind* (1960). Not a musical, the movie concerned the real-life case of a teacher accused of promoting Darwin's theory of evolution in 1925.

THE PINK PANTHER

Above: Peter Sellers and Britt Ekland who were briefly married in the 1960s. Sellers first came to prominence on BBC radio's *The Goon Show*, and began appearing in movies with fellow Goons Spike Milligan and Harry Secombe in the early '50s, before gaining recognition for his part in *The Ladykillers* (1955). He starred alongside Sophia Loren in *The Millionairess* in 1960, and became increasingly popular throughout the decade, launching his most famous and enduring character, Inspector Clouseau, in 1963's *The Pink Panther*.

Opposite: Sophia Loren in 1960 just after the release of *It Started in Naples*, in which she starred with Clark Gable.

Left: Glenn Ford in 1960. In *The Big Heat* in 1953 he had acted in a scene where scalding coffee was thrown into a victim's face, regarded as a landmark in screen violence.

A REAL HOLLYWOOD PRINCESS

Opposite and above: Grace Kelly's movie career lasted just five years, from 1951 to 1956, during which time she made only 11 movies, before she became Princess Grace of Monaco and retired from the industry. However, her body of work was impressive. She played opposite Gary Cooper in her second picture, *High Noon,* in 1952, received an Oscar nomination the following year for *Mogambo* with Clark Gable, made three Hitchcock movies whilst he was at the peak of his Hollywood career, and won Best Actress in 1954 for *The Country Girl.* She planned a return to Hollywood in the early 1960s, but her role was now that of princess, and the mood in the Principality was against it.

THE MAGNIFICENT SEVEN

Above: Newly-weds Yul and Doris Brynner in Mexico, flanked by stars of *The Magnificent Seven* (1960), including Charles Bronson (far left) and Steve McQueen (far right). The movie was based upon Akira Kurosawa's brilliant *Seven Samurai* (1954).

Opposite: Yul and Doris beginning their honeymoon in Europe in May, 1960. Although he had no movie commitments until the following year, Brynner had work to do as an ambassador for the United Nations.

Left: Following the success of *The Magnificent Seven*, Steve McQueen got top billing in *The Honeymoon Machine*. He is pictured with Paula Prentiss and Brigid Bazlen, co-stars in the picture.

BOND, JAMES BOND

Above and opposite: Connery with Honor Blackman, who was to star
opposite him as Pussy Galore in 1964's *Goldfinger*. Connery was to play Ian
Fleming's literary creation, secret agent James Bond, in the first Bond movie,
Doctor No, in 1962, and would continue to appear as 007 up until 1983.

BREAKFAST AT TIFFANY'S

Opposite: Shirley Anne Field with Steve McQueen and Robert Wagner during the filming of *The War Lover*, a 1962 drama concerning a Flying Fortress commander based in East Anglia, England, during the Second World War.

Left: Audrey Hepburn leaving a press conference following the European premiere of *Breakfast at Tiffany's* in 1961, for which she was to receive an Academy award nomination.

Above: Paul Newman and wife Joanne Woodward at London Airport. Newman had just completed filming *Exodus* on location in Cyprus.

LAWRENCE OF ARABIA

Above: Peter O'Toole with his wife Sian arriving at the premiere of
The Day They Robbed the Bank of England (1960), in which he starred. It was
produced by Jules Buck, with whom he would later form a production company.

Opposite: By 1962, O'Toole would be made world-famous by the epic
Lawrence of Arabia, which gained Best Picture, and earned him a nomination for
Best Actor.

MOORE'S BOND

Above: Roger Moore in 1962, the year he took on the role of Simon Templar in the TV series 'The Saint'. He began his career in movies as an extra in the 1940s, but is probably best known for the seven Bond pictures he made between 1972 and 1985. In the 1990s Moore began to focus on charity work, becoming UNICEF's Special Representative for the Film Arts.

Right: Jack Lemmon at a press conference prior to the premiere of *The Apartment* (1960). The movie won Best Picture and gained Billy Wilder a Best Director award. Lemmon was best known for his comedy roles in a career which stretched from the 1950s to the '90s.

Opposite: Jack Lemmon honeymooning in Rome after his marriage to actress Felicia Farr in 1962.

FONDA JUNIOR

Right: Jane Fonda, daughter of Henry, during the filming of *In the Cool of the Day* in 1962.

Opposite: A promising (American) football player at school, Shirley MacLaine's brother might have turned professional had it not been for his interest in acting. His first parts came on radio and TV, before he was cast by Elia Kazan in *Splendor in the Grass* (1960), receiving a huge fee for an unknown – $200,000. The following year he was to appear opposite Vivien Leigh in *The Roman Spring of Mrs Stone* and, seemingly out of nowhere, Warren Beatty had arrived.

CAINE'S ZULU DAWN

Above: Michael Caine pictured in the flat that he shared with Terence Stamp in 1963, the year that he got his first major movie role in *Zulu*, for which he received excellent reviews.

Opposite: American singing sensation Judy Garland pictured with British actor Dirk Bogarde in 1962. They were to appear together in *I Could Go On Singing* (1963), for which Bogarde received high praise.

FIRST BOND BEAUTY

Left: Swiss-born actress and '60s sex symbol Ursula Andress in 1964. She appeared in the first Bond movie, *Doctor No*, in 1962 as Honey Ryder, and was introduced in one of the most memorable Bond moments, emerging from the sea in a white bikini to ask Bond 'Looking for shells?' to which he replied, 'No, just looking'.

Opposite: Shaken but not stirred: Sean Connery prepares for his next scene as James Bond.

ON-SET LOVE AFFAIR

Above: Elizabeth Taylor and Richard Burton. The couple met on the set of *Cleopatra* in 1963, the most expensive movie ever made at that time, costing $35 million, but perhaps most notable for the burgeoning love affair between its two stars.

Opposite: Brigitte Bardot in 1963, the year she shocked audiences by appearing naked and reclining in the opening scene of *Contempt.*

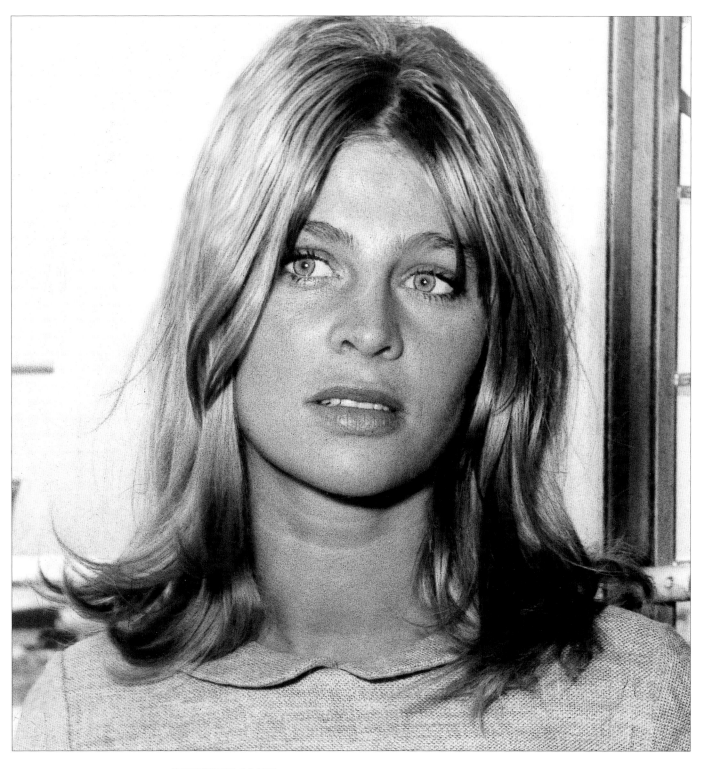

CHRISTIE'S OSCAR

Above: Julie Christie in 1964, the year after her first major film role, in *Billy Liar*, with Tom Courtenay. She received a great deal of publicity for the part, and went on to star in *Darling* with Dirk Bogarde. There had been concerns that she was too inexperienced for the role, but her performance was to win her the Oscar for Best Actress in 1965.

Opposite: Vanessa Redgrave (left), one of British theater's brightest talents during the 1960s. Redgrave moved easily into movies, receiving an Oscar nomination for her second picture, *Morgan: A Suitable Case For Treatment* (1966).

CONNERY IN DEMAND

Above: After the success of the first two Bond movies, *Doctor No* and *From Russia With Love*, Sean Connery found himself much in demand. 1964 was a busy year for the rising star, who, apart from *From Russia With Love*, made *Woman of Straw* with Gina Lollobrigida, *Goldfinger*, and Alfred Hitchcock's *Marnie*.

Opposite: Catherine Deneuve on her way to begin filming Roman Polanski's *Repulsion* in 1964. The movie itself was macabre, with Deneuve playing a neurotic murderess, but she received good notices for it and they boosted her confidence as an actress.

Right: Marlon Brando at a press conference at which he announced the formation of an international organization to boycott racial segregation within the movie and theater industries. Other famous names involved included Laurence Olivier, Vanessa Redgrave and Jean-Paul Sartre.

COMIC CURTIS

Above: Tony Curtis with Anne Ball in Paris in 1965. After playing a variety of roles, Curtis focused on comedy in the mid 1960s, with mos such as *Captain Newman*, *Wild and Wonderful*, *Goodbye Charlie* and *The Great Race*.

Opposite: Although Warren Beatty made an impact with his first two pictures, over the next few years he received little attention. That was all set to change however, in 1967, with the release of *Bonnie and Clyde*. Beatty produced and starred in the movie opposite Faye Dunaway, and although reaction in the US was initially somewhat indifferent, in Britain it was hailed as a masterpiece, prompting American critics to reassess. It went on to be a major success, bringing Beatty both fame and fortune.

ACTING PRODIGY

Left: Former child star Shirley Temple in 1965, 16 years after making her last movie, *The Story Of Seabiscuit*. In the late '50s and early '60s, she narrated and sometimes acted in her own TV series, before becoming involved in politics. She unsuccessfully ran for Congress as a Republican, before being appointed as a representative to the United Nations in 1969.

Opposite: Roger Moore has his missing cuff-links returned by stylist Isabell McMillan in 1965.

Below: Robert Redford with his wife and children in Munich with Michael Connors and his wife. The two actors were taking a break from filming *Situation Hopeless But Not Serious*, which also starred Alec Guinness.

WHAT'S IT ALL ABOUT, ALFIE?

In 1966, Michael Caine was given the lead role in the movie version of Bill Naughton's play, *Alfie*, after it had been turned down by several well-established actors. Caine received an Oscar nomination for his performance, and the picture, made on a tiny budget, was a huge success. In Britain it was second only to the latest Bond offering, *Thunderball*, and it became one of the most successful British fims at the US box-office at the time.

Right: Michael Caine in '65, the year that he was to play the part of Harry Palmer in the thriller *The Ipcress File*, which was a box-office success and confirmed Caine as a talented actor.

Opposite: Caine attending the premiere of *Alfie*, with French actress Elizabeth Ercy.

SIXTIES STYLE

Opposite: Jane Fonda in 1965, the year that she starred in the spoof western, *Cat Ballou.* Fonda was to receive seven Oscar nominations throughout her career, winning two for Best Actress in 1971's *Klute*, and 1978's *Coming Home.*

Left: Ursula Andress attracts attention even when captured off camera. In 1965 she appeared in the Woody Allen-penned *What's New Pussycat?* with Allen, Peter Sellers and Peter O'Toole.

HOLLYWOOD HEAVYWEIGHTS

Above: After his Oscar success in *The Lost Weekend* in 1945, Ray Milland was to appear in numerous less successful movies up until the 1980s. However, he continued to develop as an actor, and also proved his talents as a director with such pictures as *The Safecracker* (1958), *Panic in Year Zero* (1962) and *Hostile Witness* (1968).

Opposite: Lee Marvin received the Oscar for Best Actor for his performance in *Cat Ballou,* with Jane Fonda in 1966. Fifteen years after his debut, Marvin was now regarded as a major star, and one of the most authentic heavies in Hollywood, as he would continue to prove in *The Dirty Dozen* and *Point Blank* in 1967.

FUNNY GIRL

Opposite and above: Singer Barbra Streisand became a recording, TV and stage success, before expanding into the movie industry, being contracted for three musicals; *Funny Girl* (1968), *Hello Dolly* (1969) and *On a Clear Day You Can See Forever* (1970). She had performed in the stage version of *Funny Girl*, and the picture was to prove a huge success, earning her a $200,000 salary and a Best Actress Oscar in 1968. Unusually, the award was tied that year, with Katharine Hepburn also receiving Best Actress for *The Lion in Winter*.

Left: Yul Brynner with Yugoslavian actress Sheyla Rosin in 1968. Brynner was in Yugoslavia to film *The Battle of Nereteva*.

POITIER NOMINATED

Sidney Poitier was the first black movie star, rising to fame during the 1950s in a number of pictures which dealt with the subject of racial prejudice, such as *No Way Out* (1950), *Blackboard Jungle* (1955) and *The Defiant Ones* (1958). In the latter he played an escaped convict chained to Tony Curtis, and became the first black actor to be nominated for an Oscar for the role. He was subsequently the first black actor to win an Oscar, for 1963's *Lilies of the Field*. Poitier regarded himself first and foremost as an actor, and for a while he began to move away from race-conscious themes, but perhaps inevitably at that time, it was a subject that he would return to.

Opposite: Sidney Poitier with Suzy Kendall in 1966.

Right: James Stewart with his wife in 1967. Toward the end of his career, Stewart increasingly played the role of a father in his movies, but continued to appear in westerns such as *The Rare Breed*, *Firecreek* and *Bandolero*.

FROM TV COWBOY TO SUPERSTAR

Opposite and above: Clint Eastwood greeted by a bevy of gun-toting, poncho-wearing beauties as he promoted *A Fistful of Dollars*. Eastwood had made a name for himself as the star of TV's *Rawhide*, where he also made his first forays into scriptwriting and direction, but it was *A Fistful of Dollars* and its sequels, *For a Few Dollars More* (1966) and *The Good, the Bad and the Ugly* (1967) that brought him world-wide recognition.

MR UNIVERSE

Opposite: Arnold Schwarzenegger as a 20-year-old in 1967. Born and raised in an isolated village in Austria, he turned to body-building, and in 1968 he was to win the Mr Universe title. He moved to the US to continue to train, and soon became involved in movies, making his debut in 1970's *Hercules*.

Right: With his brooding appearance, Oliver Reed was well suited to the Hammer horror roles that first established him as an actor, but it was his role as Bill Sikes in the Oscar-winning musical *Oliver!* (1968) that brought him widespread attention. However, Reed's ability fell somewhat short of his screen presence, and he never quite managed to crack Hollywood. To some he will be best remembered as a boorish bon viveur on the chat circuit, but he continued to act until his death in 1999 while filming Ridley Scott's *Gladiator*.

AMBASSADORS

Opposite left: Raquel Welch, publicised as the American Ursula Andress, received a great deal of attention for Hammer's *One Million Years BC* (1966), but this was due largely to her fur bikini rather than to her acting ability. Her first starring role followed in *Myra Breckinridge*, with Mae West who was attempting a comeback in 1970.

Opposite right: Ursula Andress. In 1971 she was to feature in *Soleil Rouge* (Red Sun) with Charles Bronson, a western-cum-samurai movie featuring the legendary Japanese actor Toshiro Mifune.

Left: Shirley Temple on a European speaking tour as an ambassador of the American Republican party, drumming up support amongst absentee voters during the 1968 Nixon presidential campaign.

STILL LOOKING A MILLION DOLLARS

Above: The legs of retired actress and pin-up Betty Grable. Rumored to have been insured for $1 million at the height of her career, her legs are still looking a million dollars as a 52-year-old grandmother in 1969.

Left: Judi Dench on the eve of her 50th performance in *Cabaret* on the London stage. The part required her to drink a 'Prairie Oyster' in every show – a cocktail and hangover cure made from Worcestershire sauce, raw eggs and rum. Twenty years later in 1988, Dench was to begin directing plays. That same year, she was made a Dame.

Opposite: Steve McQueen had a famous passion for motor racing, a passion he was to indulge with the making of *Le Mans* (1971), which he part-financed. He is pictured on location during time trials for the Le Mans 24-hour race.

VETERAN GANGSTER

Left: Hollywood veteran Edward G Robinson, who had made his name playing gangsters, took on more lighthearted roles towards the end of his career, his last being in the sci-fi *Soylent Green* with Charlton Heston. Tragically, he died just days before its release, and a few months before being awarded an Oscar for his contribution to the movie industry.

Opposite: Long-time companions Katharine Hepburn and Spencer Tracy worked together for the last time in *Guess Who's Coming to Dinner* (1967), for which Hepburn would receive an Oscar.

Below: Princess Grace of Monaco in a replica of a room from her palace in Monaco at the Ideal Home Exhibition, London.

HITCHCOCK BACK IN LONDON

Above: Barry Foster (left) and Bernard Cribbins with Alfred Hitchcock in 1971 on the set of *Frenzy*, Hitchcock's penultimate movie.

Opposite: Julie Christie (left) with Jane Birkin and Gabrielle Crawford at Christie's home in 1971, discussing a charity performance of *Oh Calcutta!* in aid of handicapped children. That same year, Christie starred in *The Go-Between*, which won a Grand Prix at Cannes.

THE GODFATHER

When Francis Ford Coppola secured Al Pacino
the role of Michael Corleone in 1972's
The Godfather, Pacino had made just two movies,
neither of which had brought him much
attention. *The Godfather* and its sequel two years
later did, however, and his performances made
him much in demand in Hollywood. Between the
two, he made *Serpico*, the true story of a New
York cop out to expose police corruption (1973).
It was shot by Sidney Lumet, with whom Pacino
would work again on *Dog Day Afternoon* (1975),
both pictures earning him further praise, and
bringing his total Oscar nominations to four in
four years. He finally received an award for Best
Actor for his performance in *Scent of a Woman* in
1992, and continues to be eminently watchable to
this day.

DO YOU FEEL LUCKY?

Above left: Clint Eastwood was voted most popular movie star of 1970, when his portrayal of uncompromising cop Harry Callahan first hit the screen in *Dirty Harry*. The following year, he was No 1 at the box-office. The part was originally intended for Frank Sinatra, but Eastwood's performance ensured that anyone else would be almost unimaginable in the role.

Above: Having been Jerry Lewis's straight man for many years, Dean Martin became part of Frank Sinatra's 'Rat Pack' in the 1960s, making several pictures before disappearing from the silver screen around 1970.

Left: Raquel Welch in 1972. Despite off-screen arguments with Burt Reynolds during the filming of *100 Rifles* in 1969, they were to work together again in 1972 on the thriller *Fuzz*.

Opposite: Besides acting, Vanessa Redgrave was well known for her left-wing views, particularly during the 1970s, when she caused some controversy by championing the Palestinian cause. She is pictured on a protest in London.

GRADUATING

Dustin Hoffman's big break came with *The Graduate* in 1967, and the passivity of his screen character in that movie now seems somewhat typical of the roles he has played since. However, his part in *Straw Dogs* in 1971 represents a definite departure, with his character erupting into violence at the picture's climax. *Straw Dogs* tells the story of an American mathematician, played by Hoffman, and his English wife (Susan George), who move to a Cornish village in search of a quiet life. The movie was made three years before Hoffman made Lenny and two years after director Sam Peckinpah achieved box office success with *The Wild Bunch*.

Opposite: Dustin Hoffman and co-star of *Straw Dogs*, Susan George, in 1971.

Right: Hoffman on the set of *Straw Dogs*.

NEVER SAY NEVER AGAIN

Opposite: Sean Connery with his wife Diane Cilento in 1973. Two years previously Connery had starred in *Diamonds Are Forever*, the last in a series of six Bond movies that had begun with *Doctor No* in 1962. He would be back in the role in 12 years' time, however, in *Never Say Never Again*.

Above: Sidney Poitier with his partner, the Canadian actress Joanna Shimkus, and daughter Anika, on their way to Tanzania and Zambia to assess the possibilty of filming there.

Right: Well known for his roles in westerns since the beginning of his career in the 1950s, in 1973 the laconic James Coburn was to play the role of Pat Garrett in Sam Peckinpah's *Pat Garrett and Billy the Kid*.

OUTSPOKEN

Opposite: Jane Fonda in 1974. She was outspoken in her opposition to the Vietnam War during the 1970s, and in 1974 directed the documentary *Vietnam Journey*.

Above: Burt Reynolds and Dyan Cannon in *Shamus* (1974). From 1973 to 1980, Reynolds was a permanent fixture in the list of top 10 box-office attractions.

Left: Liza Minnelli dancing with Gene Kelly at the party which followed the premiere of *That's Entertainment*, a compilation of musical highlights from the studios of MGM, in which they both appear, along with a host of other stars.

BRIEF ENCOUNTER

Left: Richard Burton and Sophia Loren on location in England in 1974, filming a version of *Brief Encounter* for American TV. They also worked together on the Italian movie *Il Viaggio* (*The Trip*) that year.

Opposite: Rock Hudson made few pictures during the 1970s, but enjoyed success with the TV series *MacMillan and Wife*, and also returned to the stage. He is pictured arriving in London to appear in the musical *I Do-I Do* with Juliet Prowse.

ON GOLDEN POND

Opposite: Henry Fonda in 1975, the year that he was to star in the WWII drama, *Midway*, along with Charlton Heston, Robert Mitchum, Glenn Ford and James Coburn, amongst others. In 1982, the year of his death, he finally won the Best Actor award, for *On Golden Pond*.

Below: Lee Marvin had considered retiring from acting in 1970, but in '71 he was still in the box-office top ten, and would continue to act for another 15 years.

Left: Throughout his career, Rod Steiger was to play a number of biographical parts. From 1970 onwards, his roles ranged from Napoleon and Mussolini to W C Fields.

THE NEW BOND GIRL

Left: Britt Ekland was to join the Bond Girl club in 1975, starring with Roger Moore in *The Man With The Golden Gun*. Better known for her celebrity consorts, Ekland had, however, appeared in the cult classics *Get Carter* (1971) with Michael Caine, and *The Wicker Man* (1973) with Edward Woodward.

Right: Bound for Paris, Barbra Streisand leaves the London premiere of *Funny Lady* (1975), the sequel to the hugely successful *Funny Girl*, which had earned her an Oscar in 1968.

'ARE YOU TALKING TO ME?'

Opposite: Robert De Niro received excellent notices for his performances in Scorsese's *Mean Streets* (1973) and Coppola's *The Godfather, Part II* (1974), winning an award for Best Supporting Actor, two years after Marlon Brando had won Best Actor for the role, and the only time two actors have received Oscars for the same part. However, it was De Niro's portrayal of Travis Bickle in 1976's *Taxi Driver* (again directed by Scorsese), that really demonstrated his awesome talent.

Above: Paul Newman's famous steel-blue eyes are concealed behind dark glasses as he makes his way through London's Heathrow Airport in 1976 on his way to Milan, declaring that he was taking some time off acting. Newman's output certainly slowed around this time, but ten years later he would finally win an Oscar for Scorsese's *The Color of Money*.

LIKE FATHER LIKE SON

Opposite: Kirk Douglas's son Michael was to follow in his father's footsteps, becoming both a world-famous actor and a producer of some merit. Having abandoned hope of appearing in *One Flew Over the Cuckoo's Nest*, to which his father owned the rights, Douglas produced the movie, which swept the board at the Oscars in 1976.

Below: Michael Caine and Roger Moore encapsulated something very British in both their on and off-screen personas, but in very different ways; Moore was part of the legacy of dashing English gents, whilst Caine, with his Cockney vowels and thick glasses, seemed to represent a more down-to-earth breed of star.

Left: Michael Caine and Glenda Jackson, at the British Film Awards in 1974. Caine won Best Actor for his role in *Sleuth*, whilst Jackson won Best Actress for *A Touch of Class*.

EASY RIDER

Jack Nicholson made his first appearances in movies in the late 1950s and early '60s, and became increasingly popular up to 1969, when he was Oscar-nominated for *Easy Rider*. It was a major breakthrough, and Nicholson cemented his reputation with his performances in *Five Easy Pieces* and *Chinatown*. He was to win Best Actor for his role as Randle P McMurphy in *One Flew Over The Cuckoo's Nest*, which won five Academy Awards in total, including Best Picture, Best Director and Best Actress, which was won by Louise Fletcher, seen here with Nicholson.

HEAVEN CAN WAIT

Above: Julie Christie on her way to New York in 1976. Her career reached a peak ten years previously with David Lean's *Dr. Zhivago*, but in the 1970s she was to enjoy success with the movies she made with her lover Warren Beatty: *McCabe and Mrs Miller* (1971), *Shampoo* (1975) and *Heaven Can Wait* (1978), as well as *Don't Look Now* (1973).

Opposite: Jodie Foster in 1976 at Pinewood Studios, England, where she was making the musical gangster spoof *Bugsy Malone*, a far cry from her stark performance in Scorsese's *Taxi Driver*, which she had made the previous year, aged just 13.

BOX-OFFICE SUCCESS

Opposite: In 1978 John Travolta was to dominate the box-office with two movies, the disco-centric *Saturday Night Fever* and '50s pastiche *Grease*. Both were panned by the critics, but their success was ensured by the hordes of teeny-boppers that flocked to see them. Travolta became an overnight sensation amongst the youth, but lacked a vehicle, and perhaps the talent to carry him forward. In 1989 he made the first of the *Look Who's Talking* movies, which brought him back into the mainstream, whilst his role in Quentin Tarantino's *Pulp Fiction* in 1994 was hailed as his big comeback.

Left: Meryl Streep's first big movie was *The Deerhunter* in 1978. Considered to be a massive gamble owing to its stance on Vietnam, it went on to be a huge success, winning Best Picture and Best Director awards.

'HERE'S JOHNNY...'

In 1978 Jack Nicholson was to turn his hand to directing, making and starring in the western *Goin' South*, a sentimental, gently humorous drama. Two years later he was to star in Stanley Kubrick's chilling horror, *The Shining*, with Shelley Duvall, creating one of his most memorable characters in Jack Torrence.

Opposite: Nicholson in 1978.

Above: Jack Nicholson with Australian actress Lyndall Hobbs.

SUNDANCE KID

Opposite: Robert Redford in 1980, having appeared on the famous chat-show *Parkinson*. Redford had appeared in just one successful movie when he turned down the lead in *The Graduate* in 1967. However, two years later, he was to appear in the hugely popular *Butch Cassidy and The Sundance Kid* with Paul Newman. In 1981, he established the Sundance Institute to encourage independent movie-making.

Above: Joan Collins, 'Britain's Bad Girl'. Despite appearing in several pictures, Collins's Hollywood career never really took off, but during the 1980s she became internationally famous for her role as supreme bitch, Alexis Carrington, in TV's *Dynasty*.

SUPERMAN

Opposite and right: Christopher Reeve
had worked in theater and TV before
landing the lead in 1978's hugely popular
Superman, and although he subsequently
appeared in several other movies, it is the
role of *Superman*, in the original and its
three sequels, for which Reeve will be best
remembered and loved.

Below: Regarded as a sturdy, dependable
supporting actor, Robert Duvall did not
star in a huge number of pictures, but he
played the lead, General Dwight D
Eisenhower in *Ike: The War Years*, for
American TV in 1978.

THE PRODUCERS

Below: Comedy writer, director and actor Mel Brooks with veteran British actor, Trevor Howard. Brooks is probably best known for the Broadway satire, *The Producers* (1967) and spoof western, *Blazing Saddles* (1974), but during the 1980s he was to act as producer on some much darker movies, including David Lynch's *The Elephant Man*, and David Cronenberg's *The Fly*.

Opposite: Warren Beatty filming *Reds*. He both starred in and directed the picture, which also featured his lover, Diane Keaton, and he was to win the 1981 Best Director Oscar for his efforts.

Left: James Coburn was less active during the 1980s due to debilitating arthritis, but he continued to work, mainly in TV.

ACTOR, PRODUCER

Opposite and below: Michael Douglas relaxes in the south of France, the morning after his most recent production, *The China Syndrome*, received a standing ovation when shown in competition in Cannes, in 1978. Douglas was now well established as a producer, and would go on to have further success with his next two ventures, *Romancing the Stone* (1984) and *Jewel of the Nile* (1985), in which he also acted, alongside Danny DeVito and Kathleen Turner.

BEST PICTURE

Opposite: Sylvester Stallone on the set of *Nighthawks* in 1980. Stallone rose to fame as the star of *Rocky*, which won Best Picture and Best Director at the 1976 Oscars. Stallone had written and scripted the movie himself, claiming to have done so in a single weekend.

Above: Jack Lemmon at the Cannes film festival in 1979. Lemmon was the star of the Michael Douglas-produced, James Bridges-directed, *The China Syndrome* and was widely expected to be nominated for an Oscar for his performance.

Right: Diane Keaton had won Best Actress in 1977 for her role in Woody Allen's *Annie Hall*, but perhaps her finest performance was in *Reds*, directed by her lover at that time, Warren Beatty.

RAIN MAN

After winning the 1979 Best Actor Oscar for his performance in *Kramer vs Kramer*, Dustin Hoffman came to be regarded as one of America's best actors during the 1980s, notably for *Tootsie* (1982), for which he received an Academy nomination, and *Rain Man* (1988), with Tom Cruise, which won him the Best Actor award.

Opposite: Dustin Hoffman with girlfriend Lisa Gottsegen in 1980 in search of a play to take back to New York.

Above: Hoffman on the set of the British soap opera *Coronation Street*. Hoffman had worked with long-term *Coronation Street* director Michael Apted in 1979 on the movie *Agatha*, which also starred Vanessa Redgrave.

THE LUCK OF THE IRISH

Above: Irish-born Pierce Brosnan in the British drama-documentary *Murphy's Stroke* in 1980. That same year he made his movie debut in *The Long Good Friday*.

Left: In the tradition of Richard Burton, Welsh actor Anthony Hopkins was a man of the stage before becoming involved in movies, which he did in 1968. However, he received little notice until 1980's *The Elephant Man*.

Opposite: Sigourney Weaver and Mel Gibson on the set of Peter Weir's *The Year Of Living Dangerously* (1983). *Mad Max* star Gibson first came to the attention of Hollywood in another of Weir's pictures, *Gallipoli*, in 1981.

THE TERMINATOR

Opposite and left: Arnold
Schwarzenegger in London in
1984 to publicise his latest movie,
Conan the Destroyer, sequel to
1982's *Conan the Barbarian*,
which was hugely succesful. The
follow-up proved not to be, but
that same year Schwarzenegger
was a hit as the time-traveling
cyborg in James Cameron's slick
action sci-fi *The Terminator*.

THE JEWEL OF THE NILE

Above: Kathleen Turner first appeared in the Steve Martin comedy *The Man With Two Brains* (1983), before further successes with the comedy adventures *Romancing The Stone* (1984) and *The Jewel of the Nile* (1985).

Opposite: Robert Duvall with his wife. In 1983 he was to win the Best Actor award for his role in *Tender Mercies*.

SERIOUS ACTING

Right: Anthony Hopkins has sometimes
appeared somewhat less than discerning
with regard to the roles that he has
accepted, perhaps justified to an extent
by his disdain for the pretentiousness and
preciousness of some actors within the
profession, and refusing to take his work
completely seriously. However, it cannot
be denied that at times his acting has
approached genius.

PREMIERE LEAGUE

Opposite: Sylvester Stallone arriving in London for the premiere of *Rocky III* in 1982. As with *Rocky II* (1979), Stallone had written, directed and starred in the movie. In 1982, Stallone was also to introduce the John Rambo character with *First Blood*, which he had co-written.

Left: Despite his success with *The China Syndrome*, top roles were no longer forthcoming for Jack Lemmon, and in the '80s he worked mainly in TV. But his career was far from over and he would put in good performances in the '90s in *JFK* (1991), *Short Cuts* (1993) and *Hamlet* (1996).

REMINGTON STEELE

Opposite: Pierce Brosnan with his wife Cassandra at the opening of the musical *Chess*, staged by Tim Rice and ex-Abba men Bjorn Ulvaeus and Benny Andersson. Brosnan had become famous as the lead in TV's *Remington Steele*, a commitment that was to prevent him from accepting the role of James Bond at this time.

Left: Meryl Streep in 1985, three years after winning the Academy Award for Best Actress in *Sophie's Choice*, and the year that she would appear in the highly-praised *Out of Africa*.

PENN'S PROFILE

Left: Son of director Leo Penn and actress Eileen Ryan, Sean Penn quickly established himself with striking performances in his debut *Taps* (1981), *Fast Times at Ridgemont High* (1982) and *The Falcon and the Snowman* (1985). His profile was also raised in 1985 by his marriage to singer Madonna, with whom he was to film *Shanghai Surprise* the following year.

Opposite: Bruce Willis and soon-to-be-bride, Demi Moore. Willis found fame in 1985 through the TV series *Moonlighting*. Moore also began her career in TV, with *General Hospital*, and was soon acting in movies such as *St. Elmo's Fire* (1985).

OLD FRIENDS

Above: Diane Keaton at Cannes in 1987, where she was showing her slightly eccentric documentary *Heaven*. It was also the year that she was to appear in former partner Woody Allen's *Radio Days*.

Opposite: Denzel Washington studied journalism at university, but had always been interested in theater. He embarked on a drama scholarship after graduating, and soon landed the role of Dr Philip Chandler on the TV series *St. Elsewhere*, before gradually moving into the movie business.

FAME AND GLORY

Denzel Washington had made only three movies up to 1987, when he was to appear in the role of South African activist Steve Biko, in Richard Attenborough's *Cry Freedom*, earning him an Academy nomination for Best Supporting Actor. Following this, Washington continued to impress, receiving another Best Supporting Actor nomination in 1989 for his performance as runaway slave Trip, in Edward Zwick's Civil War movie *Glory*.

THE BIG CHILL

Kevin Costner played several small roles in the early 1980s, famously and briefly as a corpse in the opening scenes of *The Big Chill* (1983), after his part was cut. Director Lawrence Kasdan made amends by giving him a starring role in *Silverado* (1985), but it was as Eliot Ness in *The Untouchables* (1987) that he really made his mark.

Left: Costner during the making of *Dances With Wolves*, which he directed and starred in. It won Best Picture and Best Director in 1990.

Opposite above: Costner on the set of *Robin Hood: Prince of Thieves* in 1991.

Opposite below: Dame Judi Dench first took on the role of M in the Bond movie *Goldeneye* (1995), and has gone on to make it her own in *Tomorrow Never Dies* (1997), *The World is Not Enough* (1999) and *Die Another Day* (2002).

PRETTY WOMAN

Opposite: Julia Roberts initially studied journalism but then followed her brother Eric to Hollywood, where after a few movie successes that brought her to the public eye, she was to receive a nomination for Best Supporting Actress for her portrayal as Shelby in *Steel Magnolias* (1989). The following year she was to play one of her most famous parts as the prostitute Vivian Ward, opposite Richard Gere, in *Pretty Woman* (1990).

Left: Jodie Foster pictured in 1990, two years after winning Best Actress for *The Accused,* and the year before she would make her directorial debut with *Little Man Tate.*

CAREER CHANGE

Tom Cruise abandoned his original plans to become a Catholic priest to pursue a career in acting. His first movie, *Endless Love,* in 1981, was rapidly followed by a series of high-grossing pictures such as *Top Gun* (1986), *Rain Man* (1988) and *Days of Thunder* (1990), during which he was to meet his second wife, Nicole Kidman. Two years later, they would star together again in *Far and Away*.

Left: Tom Cruise and Nicole Kidman in London at the premiere of *Far and Away* (1992).

Opposite: Having made something of a recovery from the illness that had plagued him during the 1980s, James Coburn began to take on more work in the '90s, and in 1998 he won an Oscar for his role in *Affliction*. He is pictured with his wife Paula.

MYSTIC RIVER

Opposite and right: Sean Penn at the Cannes film festival. Penn did nothing to improve his reputation as an angry and volatile young man by assaulting a journalist in 1987, for which he received a six-month jail term. However, the incident did not adversely affect his reviews, or his reputation as a consistently good actor. If anything it seemed to confirm a rebelliousness reminiscent of James Dean or Marlon Brando. It was an intensity that he was to bring to many of his performances throughout the 1980s and '90s, and in 2003 he won Best Actor for *Mystic River*.

TOP SUPPORT

Above: Robert Duvall continued as a supporting actor throughout the 1990s, appearing in such movies as *Days of Thunder* (1990), *Falling Down* (1993) and *Deep Impact* (1998). But he was also to write, direct and star in *The Apostle* (1997), which was highly acclaimed.

Opposite: International success came to French actor Gérard Depardieu after his roles in *Cyrano de Bergerac* (1989) and *Green Card* (1990).

RISING STAR

Born in Wales, Catherine Zeta-Jones first came to the public eye for her role as Mariette in the British television drama *The Darling Buds of May* in 1991. Her first movie success was as Elena, playing opposite Anthony Hopkins, in *The Mask of Zorro* in 1998. *Entrapment* and *The Haunting* followed a year later.

Left: Catherine Zeta-Jones on the set of *The Darling Buds of May*.

Opposite: Zeta-Jones at a photo call for TV drama *Out of the Blue*, in 1991.

Below: Warren Beatty lived a long life as a bachelor, dating numerous leading ladies, but in 1992 he finally married actress Annette Bening. They met whilst filming *Bugsy* (1991).

FAR AND AWAY

In 1990, Tom Cruise had received a Best Actor Oscar nomination for his role as Vietnam veteran Ron Kovic in Oliver Stone's *Born on the Fourth of July*, and he followed this success with excellent performances in *A Few Good Men* (1992), best remembered for its climactic scenes with Cruise and Jack Nicholson, and *The Firm* (1993).

Left: Tom Cruise and Nicole Kidman in 1992, in advance of the premiere of *Far and Away*.

Opposite: Cruise and Kidman in 1993.

RUN OF SUCCESS

Left: Julia Roberts in 1992. Following *Pretty Woman*, Julia Roberts continued to star in many successful movies including *The Pelican Brief* (1993), *My Best Friend's Wedding* (1997), and *Notting Hill* (1999), where she showed her ability to play romantic comedy roles.

Opposite: Kathleen Turner with Sir Ian McKellen at the Laurence Olivier Awards in 1992. A star of the stage since the early 1960s, Ian McKellen has become something of a British institution. He moved into movies in the late '60s and has since proved himself to be a remarkable screen actor. He was knighted in 1991, and most recently has appeared as Gandalf in Peter Jackson's Lord of the Rings trilogy.

DEPARDIEU'S PERIOD PIECES

Left: Gérard Depardieu has featured in several modern roles, but seems to favor, and appear most comfortable in, period pieces, be they fictional or historical. He has played characters such as Balzac, Jean Valjean, the Count of Monte Cristo, Porthos, and Columbus. He is pictured with his wife, attending the premiere of Ridley Scott's *1492: Conquest of Paradise* in 1992.

Opposite: Denzel Washington pictured in 1992, soon after he had completed filming the life story of the militant black activist Malcom X.

A GREAT SCREEN VILLAIN

Left: In 1991 Anthony Hopkins was to play Hannibal Lecter in *The Silence of the Lambs,* and whilst the character had been brought to the screen before, in Michael Mann's *Manhunter,* and Hopkins no doubt played it with a little more humor, his performance was regarded by many as one of the greatest portrayals of screen villainy, and it earned him the Oscar for Best Actor.

Opposite and above: Typically larger than life both on and off screen, Burt Reynolds has not always been taken seriously as an actor, but he has been consistently popular, and holds an award for being the No 1 box-office star for five consecutive years. He is also well known for his philanthropy, developing educational and entertainment venues, including the Burt Reynolds Institute of Theater Training, and an outreach program for young actors.

HARD ROCK

Above: Sylvester Stallone arriving at the 21st-anniversary celebrations for London's Hard Rock Cafe in 1992 with girlfriend Jennifer Flavin. Other celebrities in attendance included George Harrison and Prince. Stallone was in Britain planning a London branch of his movie memorabilia themed eaterie, Planet Hollywood.

Opposite: Arnold Schwarzenegger and his wife attending a party in 1992, the year after his greatest success, *Terminator 2*.

PLANET HOLLYWOOD

Right: Screen hard-men, Sylvester Stallone,
Arnold Schwarzenegger and Bruce Willis came
together in 1992 to launch restaurant and
movie shrine Planet Hollywood.
Schwarzenegger's Harley-Davidson from the
Terminator picture was amongst the movie
memorabilia on display. Willis's first role as a
tough-guy came in 1988, playing John McLane
in *Die Hard*, which spawned two successful
sequels; *Die Hard 2* (1990), and *Die Hard: With
a Vengeance* (1995). Action roles aside, Willis
has gone on to show greater range and talent
in such pictures as Quentin Tarantino's *Pulp
Fiction* (1994), *The Sixth Sense* (1999) and
Unbreakable (2000).

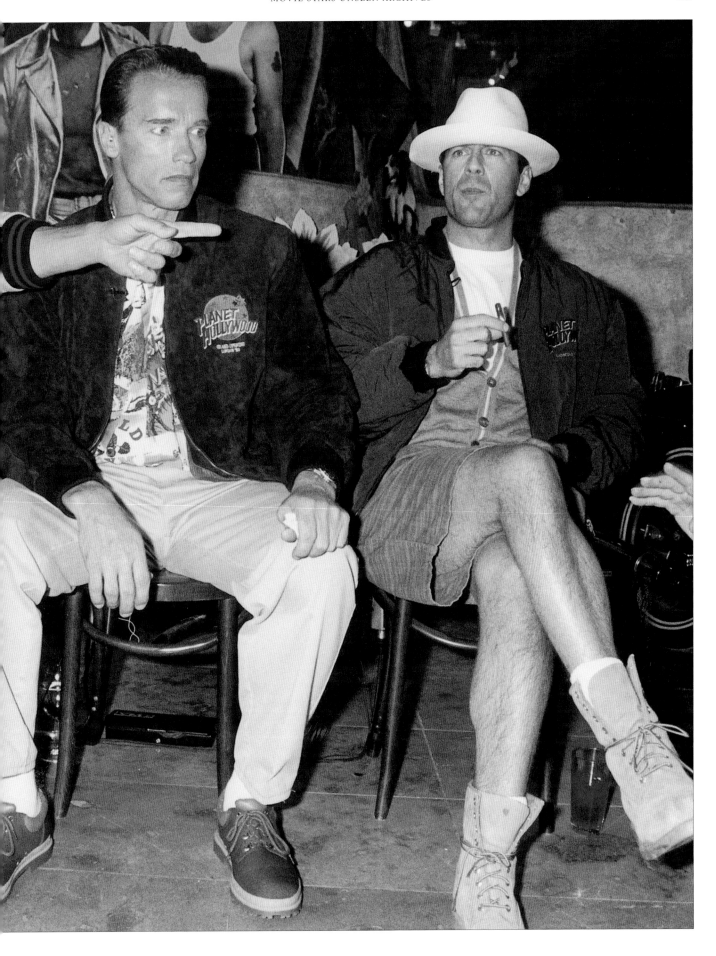

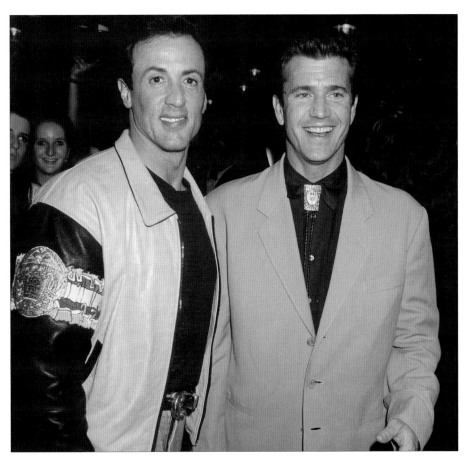

'TINSELTOWN ON THAMES'

Below: Sylvester Stallone, Arnold Schwarzenegger and Bruce Willis at the opening of London's Planet Hollywood. Willis, who arrived with his wife Demi Moore, described the restaurant as 'Tinseltown on Thames'. Schwarzenegger meanwhile, revealed that his mother supplied the recipe for their apple strudel.

Left: Sylvester Stallone with Mel Gibson at the launch party. Other guests included Michael J Fox, Christopher Reeve, Johnny Depp and Charlie Sheen.

Opposite: Sylvester Stallone arriving with girlfriend Jennifer Flavin, whom he would marry in 1997.

EDWARD SCISSORHANDS

Above: Johnny Depp arrives at the Planet Hollywood opening. Depp initially carved a career as a musician, but became involved in acting after meeting Nicolas Cage. Depp's debut was in *Nightmare on Elm Street* (1984), which was followed by a part in *21 Jump Street*, the TV series that made him famous. He was then to appear in *Edward Scissorhands* in 1990, the first of many collaborations with director Tim Burton.

Opposite: Halle Berry was initially noted for winning several American beauty contests and soon broke into the world of modeling, before gaining parts on TV's *Knots Landing* and *Living Dolls*. Her first movie was Spike Lee's *Jungle Fever* in 1991, when she played the part of a crack addict. Berry reportedly took a method-actor approach, refusing to bathe for several days before filming, to enhance her performance.

A REAL SUPERHERO

Best known in his role as the hero
Superman, Christopher Reeve was
to become a real hero after a
riding accident in 1995 left him
paralyzed. Determined to walk
again, he became a campaigner for
spinal injury research and
managed to continue working
from time to time before his tragic
death on 10th October 2004.

Opposite: Christopher Reeve in
1993.

Right: Reeve with his wife Dana.

DIE HARD

The role of John McLane in *Die Hard* was originally offered to 'The Italian Stallion', Sylvester Stallone, who turned the part down. It was taken up instead by Bruce Willis, who was to have major success with the part.

Left: Bruce Willis leaves London's Dorchester Hotel on his way to Planet Hollywood.

Opposite: Willis with his wife Demi Moore at the Planet Hollywood party.

Below: Willis and Moore pictured with Johnny Depp.

GOING SOLO

Left: Harrison Ford shot to fame as Han Solo in 1977's *Star Wars*, returning in the same role in the sequels; *The Empire Strikes Back* (1980) and *Return of the Jedi* (1983). He continued his success with the Indiana Jones movies, beginning with *Raiders of the Lost Ark* in 1981, and has had starring roles in four of the ten highest-grossing movies of all time. He was to receive a Golden Globe nomination for *The Fugitive*, which opened in 1993.

Opposite: After attending Yale Drama School, Sigourney Weaver landed herself the part of Ripley in *Alien* in 1978, and after three sequels, it is probably the role that she is most readily associated with. However, it was *Gorillas in the Mist* that would bring critical acclaim, earning her a Best Actress nomination in 1988.

CLEAN-CUT IMAGE

Opposite: By the mid-1990s, Tom Cruise was one of the highest-paid and most respected actors in Hollywood, renowned for his compassion and generosity. A departure from his usual, clean-cut roles, in 1994 Cruise was to star in *Interview with the Vampire*, alongside Brad Pitt and a 12-year-old Kirsten Dunst.

Right: In 1994, Tom Hanks won Best Actor for his portrayal of an AIDS sufferer in *Philadelphia*, and went on to win the award the following year for *Forrest Gump*, the first actor to win in successive years since Spencer Tracy in 1937 and 1938.

Above: 1993 was to prove a successful year for Anthony Hopkins. He was both knighted and received an Oscar nomination for *Remains of the Day*.

MEAN STREETS

Left: Considered to be one of the best actors of his generation, De Niro has played a wealth of characters with both charisma and formidable authority. He first established his style in Martin Scorsese's *Mean Streets* in 1973. Since then he has received five Oscar nominations, winning two for Best Actor: *The Godfather Part II* in 1974 and *Raging Bull* in 1980. Further nominations for Best Actor were received for *The Deer Hunter* (1978), *Cape Fear* and *Awakenings* (1991). De Niro has his own production company called Tribeca Film Center and made his directorial debut in 1993 with *A Bronx Tale*. He is pictured at the British Film Awards in 1994.

Opposite: Johnny Depp with girlfriend and model Kate Moss in 1994. Between '93 and '94 Depp was to make no less than four movies: *Benny & Joon*, *What's Eating Gilbert Grape*, *Ed Wood* and *Arizona Dream*.

BRAVEHEART

Opposite: Mel Gibson became a huge name in Hollywood with *Lethal Weapon* (1987) and its sequels, but his personal triumph came with 1995's *Braveheart*, which he both directed and starred in. It won Best Picture and earned him Best Director.

Above: Bruce Willis makes a guest appearance behind the bar at Planet Hollywood in 1994. He was well qualified for the job, having worked as a bar-tender before his big break in acting.

Left: Bruce Willis and Demi Moore with Jon Bon Jovi and his wife at Planet Hollywood.

FOUR WEDDINGS

Above: Hugh Grant was still a university undergraduate when he made his screen debut in *Privileged* (1982), before appearing in E M Forster's *Maurice* in 1987, which earned him international recognition. The same year Grant set up production company Simian Films with girlfriend Elizabeth Hurley, a venture that was to continue after their eventual separation. His major breakthrough came in 1994 with *Four Weddings and a Funeral*.

Opposite: Hugh Grant and Elizabeth Hurley at the premiere of *Four Weddings and a Funeral*. Hurley's dress stole the show.

Right: Grant at the premiere of *An Awfully Big Adventure* (1995).

GOLDENEYE

Opposite and above: In 1995, Pierce Brosnan was to make his debut as James Bond, in *Goldeneye*. He had been offered the role many years earlier, but had had to turn it down due to work commitments in his role as TV's *Remington Steele*. Brosnan continued to play Bond, starring in *Tomorrow Never Dies* in 1997, *The World is Not Enough* in 1999 and *Die Another Day* in 2002.

LEADING MAN

In 1996, Tom Cruise was nominated for Best Actor, this time for his performance in *Jerry Maguire*, the same year in which he starred in *Mission Impossible*. Another nomination followed in 1999 for Best Supporting Actor in *Magnolia*. He has continued to be a big box-office draw, starring in such movies as *Vanilla Sky* (2001), *Minority Report* (2002), *The Last Samurai* (2003) and *Collateral* (2004).

Opposite and left: Tom Cruise greeting fans at the London premiere of *Interview with the Vampire*, in January 1995. Cruise has been known to spend over an hour on the red carpet at such occasions, chatting, signing autographs and on one well publicised occasion, phoning a fan's mother, who was too busy to take the call!

TITANIC BREAKTHROUGH

Kate Winslet made her movie debut in Peter Jackson's *Heavenly Creatures* (1994), going on to receive an Oscar nomination the following year for *Sense and Sensibility*, and to star in the blockbuster *Titanic* in 1997. A further nomination for Best Actress gave her the accolade of being the youngest actress to receive two Oscar nominations. Recent successes have included *The Life of David Gale* (2003) and *Finding Neverland* (2004).

Opposite: Kate Winslet after she secured the role in *Heavenly Creatures*, aged just 17.

Above: Winslet in 1996, the year before the huge success of *Titanic.*

BRAD'S BREAK

After moving to Los Angeles in 1986, Brad Pitt took on a variety of jobs to pay for acting lessons. His movie breakthrough came in 1991 when he appeared as the lanky cowboy JD in *Thelma and Louise*. Although on screen for only fourteen minutes the character launched his career. Further successes followed, most notably, *Seven* and *Twelve Monkeys* in 1995 for which he earned an Oscar nomination for Best Supporting Actor.

Left: He is pictured in 1996 with his girlfriend at that time, Gwyneth Paltrow.

Opposite: Johnny Depp with Kate Moss at a concert in London's Finsbury Park, 1996.

THE USUAL SUSPECTS

Opposite: Kevin Spacey made his movie debut in *Heartburn* in 1986 and then began to play a string of dark and sinister characters, including the creepy eye-witness Verbal Kint in *The Usual Suspects* in 1995, winning him an Oscar for Best Supporting Actor. The same year he appeared in the thriller *Seven*, refusing to appear on the billing so that the picture's ending would not be compromised. Spacey made his directorial debut with *Albino Alligator* in 1997, and in 1999 his appearance in *American Beauty* earned him another Oscar, for Best Actor.

Above: Initially signed to Warner Bros, George Clooney played several small supporting roles before coming to the public eye in the 1990s in the highly successful television series *ER*. Major movie parts quickly followed with lead roles in *One Fine Day* and *From Dusk Till Dawn* in 1996.

BEST ACTRESS

Opposite: Gwyneth Paltrow made her first appearance in the movies in 1991 when she was cast in both *Shout* and *Hook*. Other parts followed, and she made a major breakthrough playing Emma Woodhouse in *Emma* (1996), closely followed by Viola in *Shakespeare in Love*. It was for this performance, directed by John Madden, that she received an Oscar for Best Actress in 1998. The following year she played Marge Sherwood in *The Talented Mr Ripley* and in 2003 took the lead role of Sylvia Plath in *Sylvia*, directed by Christine Jeffs.

Left: Sigourney Weaver attending The British Academy Film Awards in 1998, the year after her outstanding performance in *The Ice Storm*.

DANCING TALENT

Opposite: In 2002, Catherine Zeta-Jones was awarded the Oscar for Best Supporting Actress in *Chicago*, a movie where she was able to use her dancing talents playing Velma Kelly. Two years later she appeared in Steven Soderbergh's *Ocean's Twelve*.

Left: Before *Chicago*, Catherine Zeta-Jones had demonstrated her musical talents, starring in the Kurt Weill opera *Street Scene* at the London Coliseum in 1989.

SMASH HITS

Opposite: Hugh Grant stepping out with his girlfriend, Elizabeth Hurley. In 1994 Grant appeared in the immensely succcessful *Four Weddings and a Funeral*, receiving a BAFTA Award for Best Actor. The following year he appeared in *Sense and Sensibility* and in 1995 co-starred with Julia Roberts in *Notting Hill*, another British smash hit. Grant's portrayal as the charming but caddish Daniel Cleaver in *Bridget Jones's Diary* followed two years later and its popularity at the box-office led to the sequel in 2004.

Left: Brad Pitt's popularity grew throughout the 1990s through parts in *A River Runs Through It* (1992), *True Romance* (1993), *Seven* and *Twelve Monkeys* (1995), and *Fight Club* (1999). Accordingly, Pitt's salary has also grown, from just $6000 for his part in *Thelma and Louise*, to more than $17 million for the lead role in 2004's *Troy*. He is pictured in 1995 with fellow actor Henry Thomas.

MAN IN BLACK

Will Smith originally pursued a career in music until he was given a part in the sitcom *The Fresh Prince of Bel-Air*. This highly successful television series lasted for six years during which he began to be offered parts in movies. The first, 1993's *Six Degrees of Separation*, was soon followed by the highly-acclaimed *Independence Day* (1996). He was cast as Agent J in the first of three *Men in Black* films in 1997, and went on to receive an Oscar nomination for his part in *Ali* in 2002.

Right: Will Smith performing at a concert in 1998.

Opposite above: George Clooney with his then girlfriend Celine Balitran and Arnold Schwarzenegger with his wife Maria Shriver at the London premiere of *Batman and Robin* in 1997.

Opposite below: Michael Douglas pictured with actress Catherine Zeta-Jones in 1999. The couple married the following year.

LARA CROFT

The daughter of actor Jon Voight, Angelina Jolie trained in the theater, was an international model and performed in music videos before breaking into the world of film. Her first major part was in *Hackers* (1995), but it was for her role in *Gia* (1998), that she caught the public's attention. In 1999 she portrayed Lisa Rowe in *Girl, Interrupted* gaining an Oscar for Best Supporting Actress. She played the lead in *Lara Croft: Tomb Raider* in 2001, and again in the sequel two years later.

Above: Angelina Jolie filming *Tomb Raider: The Cradle of Life*.

Opposite: Jolie arriving at the premiere of *Gone in Sixty Seconds*, in which she starred in 2000.

Left: Kate Winslet announcing the nomination shortlist for the 51st British Academy Film Awards in 1999.

GLADIATOR

Above: Russell Crowe promoting his movie *Proof of Life* in 2000, which also starred Meg Ryan. New Zealand-born Crowe made his first picture, *Romper Stomper* in 1992, and was soon to catch America's eye. He was sought out by Sharon Stone for *The Quick and the Dead* (1995), but his first major hit was 1997's *L A Confidential*. In 2000 he won an Oscar for Best Actor in the movie *Gladiator*, and received a nomination the following year for his role in *A Beautiful Mind*.

Opposite below: Matt Damon, Jude Law, Gwyneth Paltrow and Jack Davenport, stars of *The Talented Mr Ripley*, at the party which followed the movie's premiere. Law trained in theater before gaining a part in the TV soap *Families* in 1990. He began his stage career in 1992, and was nominated for the Olivier Award for Outstanding Newcomer, before his first major movie success with *Gattaca* in 1997. He has received two Best Actor nominations, for *The Talented Mr Ripley* (1999) and *Cold Mountain* (2003).

Opposite above: Matt Damon following the premiere of *The Talented Mr Ripley*.

DIE ANOTHER DAY

Left: Pierce Brosnan with leading ladies Halle Berry (right) and Rosamund Pike at the photocall promoting the latest James Bond movie, *Die Another Day*, in 2002. The working title for the picture was simply, Bond 20.

Opposite: Halle Berry earned huge praise for her performance in the TV series *Roots* in 1993 and Warren Beatty's *Bulworth* in 1998. In 2000 she featured as Storm in *X-Men* and again in the sequel *X-Men 2* three years later. She received an Oscar for Best Actress playing Leticia Musgrove in *Monster's Ball* (2001), and went on to star in *Die Another Day* in 2002. Further success came in the lead role in *Catwoman* two years later. She is pictured arriving at the premiere of the Star Wars movie, *Episode II: Attack of the Clones*, in 2002.

MILLION DOLLAR ACTING

Born in Tennessee in the 1930s, Morgan Freeman initially joined the US Air Force as a mechanic. He gradually began to work in television in the seventies and took on minor movie roles in the eighties. His first major break was in *Street Smart* in 1987 when he received the first of four Oscar nominations; on this occasion for Best Supporting Actor. Two years later he played the role of the chauffeur Hoke Colburn in *Driving Miss Daisy*, and was again nominated for Best Supporting Actor. He was cast as Azeem in *Robin Hood: Prince of Thieves* (1991), before receiving his nomination for Best Actor for his portrayal of Ellis Boyd 'Red' Redding in *The Shawshank Redemption* in 1994. Freeman finally won an Oscar for Best Supporting Actor when he teamed up with Clint Eastwood to play Eddie 'Scrap-Iron' Dupris in *Million Dollar Baby* in 2005.

OCEAN'S ELEVEN

A highly versatile actor, Samuel L Jackson spent the eighties playing a variety of character roles in television and on stage until he appeared as a crack addict in *Jungle Fever* in 1991. The role earned him a special acting prize at the Cannes Film Festival and from then on his career and popularity soared. Two years later the role of Jules Winnfield the mercurial hit man in *Pulp Fiction* earned him an Oscar nomination for Best Supporting Actor. A string of highly acclaimed titles followed, including the long- awaited *Star Wars: Episode 1: The Phantom Menace*, in which he was to play the coveted role of Mace Windu, a character he continued to portray in further episodes.

Opposite: Samuel L Jackson arrives at the premiere of Paramount's *Coach Carter* (2005), in Los Angeles.

Left: George Clooney took on the Batman role in 1997's *Batman and Robin*, starred in *The Perfect Storm* in 2000, and then played Danny Ocean in *Ocean's Eleven* in 2001. He was also executive-producer for the sequel *Ocean's Twelve*, three years later. He is pictured at the premiere of *The Perfect Storm*.

JOHNNY AND VANESSA

Opposite: Ewan McGregor's first major part was in the TV serialisation of Dennis Potter's *Lipstick on Your Collar* in 1993, but it was his role in Danny Boyle's *Trainspotting* (1996), that really brought him to the public eye. Since then he has remained a highly acclaimed actor, appearing in *Little Voice* (1998) and alongside Nicole Kidman in *Moulin Rouge* (2001). One of his most renowned parts is as Obi-Wan Kenobi in the recent *Star Wars* movies.

Left: Johnny Depp and wife Vanessa Paradis arrive at the 11th Annual Screen Actors Guild Awards at the Shrine Exposition Center, Los Angeles, California, 2005. Depp has received two Oscar nominations for Best Actor. The first for *Pirates of the Caribbean: The Curse of the Black Pearl* in 2004 and the following year for *Finding Neverland* when he played Sir James Matthew Barrie, author of *Peter Pan*.

A TITANIC STAR

Opposite: Encouraged into acting by his parents, Leonardo DiCaprio had his movie breakthrough in 1993 with *This Boy's Life* when he played alongside Robert de Niro. The following year he received a nomination for Best Supporting Actor in *What's Eating Gilbert Grape*, playing the mentally-retarded brother to Johnny Depp's Gilbert. His role as Romeo in *Romeo and Juliet* (1996) soon followed and in 1997 James Cameron's blockbuster *Titanic* arrived at the box-office with DiCaprio cast as Jack Dawson opposite Kate Winslet. The movie was to receive fourteen Oscar nominations, winning eleven of these, and DiCaprio became an international phenomenon. More recently he received a further Oscar nomination for Best Actor for his portrayal of the eccentric millionaire Howard Hughes in *The Aviator* (2004). He is pictured at a ceremony in Paris, 2005, where he was awarded the Chevalier of Arts and Literature medal by the French Culture Minister.

Right: Uma Thurman's first major movie role came in 1988's *Dangerous Liaisons*, and she was later to take the industry by storm, donning a short black wig to play the sly and smoldering Mia Wallace in Quentin Tarantino's *Pulp Fiction*, for which she earned an Oscar nomination for Best Supporting Actress. Two lavish period dramas, *The Golden Bowl* and *Vatel* were both highly acclaimed at the Cannes Film Festival in 2000 and she was to work with Tarantino again in *Kill Bill*: Vol 1 and 2 (2003 & 2004) playing the main character of the Bride. She is pictured at a fashion show in New York.

MOST SOUGHT AFTER

Opposite: In 2001, Julia Roberts won an Oscar for Best Actress in *Erin Brockovich*, directed by Steven Soderbergh. She was to appear in two further movies under his direction, *Ocean's Eleven* (2001) and the sequel *Ocean's Twelve* (2004). She is pictured attending the world premiere of *Mona Lisa Smile* in December 2003, at New York's Ziegfeld Theater.

Left: As a Franciscan seminary student at the age of fourteen, Tom Cruise could have had no idea that in a relatively short space of time he would become one of the highest-paid, best-liked and most sought-after actors in Hollywood, and regarded as one of the 100 greatest movie stars of all time.

The Oscars
Best Actor and Best Actress

1928
Best Actor: Emil Jannings
(The Last Command and
The Way of All Flesh)
Best Actress: Janet Gaynor
(Seventh Heaven, Street Angel
and Sunrise)

1929
Best Actor: Warner Baxter
(In Old Arizona)
Best Actress: Mary Pickford
(Coquette)

1930
Best Actor: George Arliss
(Disraeli)
Best Actress: Norma Shearer
(The Divorcee)

1931
Best Actor: Lionel Barrymore
(A Free Soul)
Best Actress: Marie Dressler
(Min and Bill)

1932
Best Actor: tie between Fredric March
(Dr Jekyll and Mr Hyde)
and Wallace Beery
(The Champ)
Best Actress: Helen Hayes
(The Sin of Madelon Claudet)

1933
Best Actor: Charles Laughton
(The Private Life of Henry VIII)
Best Actress: Katharine Hepburn
(Morning Glory)

1934
Best Actor: Clark Gable
(It Happened One Night)
Best Actress: Claudette Colbert
(It Happened One Night)

1935
Best Actor: Victor McLaglen
(The Informer)
Best Actress: Bette Davis
(Dangerous)

1936
Best Actor: Paul Muni
(The Story of Louis Pasteur)
Best Actress: Luise Rainer
(The Great Ziegfeld)

1937
Best Actor: Spencer Tracy
(Captains Courageous)
Best Actress: Luise Rainer
(The Good Earth)

1938
Best Actor: Spencer Tracy
(Boys' Town)
Best Actress: Bette Davis
(Jezebel)

1939
Best Actor: Robert Donat
(Goodbye, Mr Chips)
Best Actress: Vivien Leigh
(Gone with the Wind)

1940
Best Actor: James Stewart
(The Philadelphia Story)
Best Actress: Ginger Rogers
(Kitty Foyle)

1941
Best Actor: Gary Cooper
(Sergeant York)
Best Actress: Joan Fontaine
(Suspicion)

1942
Best Actor: James Cagney
(Yankee Doodle Dandy)
Best Actress: Greer Garson
(Mrs Miniver)

1943
Best Actor: Paul Lukas
(Watch on the Rhine)
Best Actress: Jennifer Jones
(The Song of Bernadette)

1944
Best Actor: Bing Crosby
(Going My Way)
Best Actress: Ingrid Bergman
(Gaslight)

1945
Best Actor: Ray Milland
(The Lost Weekend)
Best Actress: Joan Crawford
(Mildred Pierce)

1946
Best Actor: Fredric March
(The Best Years of Our Lives)
Best Actress: Olivia de Havilland
(To Each His Own)

1947
Best Actor: Ronald Colman
(A Double Life)
Best Actress: Loretta Young
(The Farmer's Daughter)

1948
Best Actor: Laurence Olivier
(Hamlet)
Best Actress: Jane Wyman
(Johnny Belinda)

1949
Best Actor: Broderick Crawford
(All the King's Men)
Best Actress: Olivia de Havilland
(The Heiress)

1950
Best Actor: José Ferrer
(Cyrano de Bergerac)
Best Actress: Judy Holliday
(Born Yesterday)

1951
Best Actor: Humphrey Bogart
(The African Queen)
Best Actress: Vivien Leigh
(A Streetcar Named Desire)

1952
Best Actor: Gary Cooper
(High Noon)
Best Actress: Shirley Booth
(Come Back, Little Sheba)

1953
Best Actor: William Holden
(Stalag 17)
Best Actress: Audrey Hepburn
(Roman Holiday)

1954
Best Actor: Marlon Brando
(On the Waterfront)
Best Actress: Grace Kelly
(The Country Girl)

1955
Best Actor: Ernest Borgnine
(Marty)
Best Actress: Anna Magnani
(The Rose Tattoo)

1956
Best Actor: Yul Brynner
(The King and I)
Best Actress: Ingrid Bergman
(Anastasia)

1957
Best Actor: Alec Guinness
(The Bridge on the River Kwai)
Best Actress: Joanne Woodward
(The Three Faces of Eve)

1958
Best Actor: David Niven
(Separate Tables)
Best Actress: Susan Hayward
(I Want to Live!)

1959
Best Actor: Charlton Heston
(Ben-Hur)
Best Actress: Simone Signoret
(Room at the Top)

1960
Best Actor: Burt Lancaster
(Elmer Gantry)
Best Actress: Elizabeth Taylor
(Butterfield 8)

1961
Best Actor: Maximilian Schell
(Judgment at Nuremberg)
Best Actress: Sophia Loren
(Two Women)

1962
Best Actor: Gregory Peck
(To Kill a Mockingbird)
Best Actress: Anne Bancroft
(The Miracle Worker)

1963
Best Actor: Sidney Poitier
(Lilies of the Field)
Best Actress: Patricia Neal (Hud)

1964
Best Actor: Rex Harrison
(My Fair Lady)
Best Actress: Julie Andrews
(Mary Poppins)

1965
Best Actor: Lee Marvin
(Cat Ballou)
Best Actress: Julie Christie
(Darling)

1966
Best Actor: Paul Scofield
(A Man for All Seasons)
Best Actress: Elizabeth Taylor
(Who's Afraid of Virginia Woolf?)

1967
Best Actor: Rod Steiger
(In the Heat of the Night)
Best Actress: Katharine Hepburn
(Guess Who's Coming to Dinner)

1968
Best Actor: Cliff Robertson
(Charly)
Best Actress: tie between
Katharine Hepburn
(The Lion in Winter)
and Barbra Streisand
(Funny Girl)

1969
Best Actor: John Wayne
(True Grit)
Best Actress: Maggie Smith
(The Prime of Miss Jean Brodie)

1970
Best Actor: George C Scott
(Patton)
Best Actress: Glenda Jackson
(Women in Love)

1971
Best Actor: Gene Hackman
(The French Connection)
Best Actress: Jane Fonda
(Klute)

1972
Best Actor: Marlon Brando
(The Godfather)
Best Actress: Liza Minnelli
(Cabaret)

1973
Best Actor: Jack Lemmon
(Save the Tiger)
Best Actress: Glenda Jackson
(A Touch of Class)

1974
Best Actor: Art Carney
(Harry and Tonto)
Best Actress: Ellen Burstyn
(Alice Doesn't Live Here Any More)

1975
Best Actor: Jack Nicholson
(One Flew Over the Cuckoo's Nest)
Best Actress: Louise Fletcher
(One Flew Over the Cuckoo's Nest)

1976
Best Actor: Peter Finch
(Network)
Best Actress: Faye Dunaway
(Network)

1977
Best Actor: Richard Dreyfuss
(The Goodbye Girl)
Best Actress: Diane Keaton
(Annie Hall)

1978
Best Actor: Jon Voight
(Coming Home)
Best Actress: Jane Fonda
(Coming Home)

1979
Best Actor: Dustin Hoffman
(Kramer vs. Kramer)
Best Actress: Sally Field
(Norma Rae)

1980
Best Actor: Robert De Niro
(Raging Bull)
Best Actress: Sissy Spacek
(Coal Miner's Daughter)

1981
Best Actor: Henry Fonda
(On Golden Pond)
Best Actress: Katharine Hepburn
(On Golden Pond)

1982
Best Actor: Ben Kingsley
(Gandhi)
Best Actress: Meryl Streep
(Sophie's Choice)

1983
Best Actor: Robert Duvall
(Tender Mercies)
Best Actress: Shirley MacLaine
(Terms of Endearment)

1984
Best Actor: F Murray Abraham
(Amadeus)
Best Actress: Sally Field
(Places in the Heart)

1985
Best Actor: William Hurt
(Kiss of the Spider Woman)
Best Actress: Geraldine Page
(The Trip to Bountiful)

1986
Best Actor: Paul Newman
(The Color of Money)
Best Actress: Marlee Matlin
(Children of a Lesser God)

1987
Best Actor: Michael Douglas
(Wall Street)
Best Actress: Cher
(Moonstruck)

1988
Best Actor: Dustin Hoffman
(Rain Man)
Best Actress: Jodie Foster
(The Accused)

1989
Best Actor: Daniel Day-Lewis
(My Left Foot)
Best Actress: Jessica Tandy
(Driving Miss Daisy)

1990
Best Actor: Jeremy Irons
(Reversal of Fortune)
Best Actress: Kathy Bates
(Misery)

1991
Best Actor: Anthony Hopkins
(The Silence of the Lambs)
Best Actress: Jodie Foster
(The Silence of the Lambs)

1992
Best Actor: Al Pacino
(Scent of a Woman)
Best Actress: Emma Thompson
(Howards End)

1993
Best Actor: Tom Hanks
(Philadelphia)
Best Actress: Holly Hunter
(The Piano)

1994
Best Actor: Tom Hanks
(Forrest Gump)
Best Actress: Jessica Lange
(Blue Sky)

1995
Best Actor: Nicolas Cage
(Leaving Las Vegas)
Best Actress: Susan Sarandon
(Dead Man Walking)

1996
Best Actor: Geoffrey Rush
(Shine)
Best Actress: Frances McDormand
(Fargo)

1997
Best Actor: Jack Nicholson
(As Good As It Gets)
Best Actress: Helen Hunt
(As Good As It Gets)

1998
Best Actor: Roberto Benigni
(Life is Beautiful)
Best Actress: Gwyneth Paltrow
(Shakespeare in Love)

1999
Best Actor: Kevin Spacey
(American Beauty)
Best Actress: Hilary Swank
(Boys Don't Cry)

2000
Best Actor: Russell Crowe
(Gladiator)
Best Actress: Julia Roberts
(Erin Brockovich)

2001
Best Actor: Denzel Washington
(Training Day)
Best Actress: Halle Berry
(Monster's Ball)

2002
Best Actor: Adrien Brody
(The Pianist)
Best Actress: Nicole Kidman
(The Hours)

2003
Best Actor: Sean Penn
(Mystic River)
Best Actress: Charlize Theron
(Monster)

2004
Best Actor: Jamie Foxx
(Ray)
Best Actress: Hilary Swank
(Million Dollar Baby)

Index

A

Aadland, Beverly   112
Amanda, Lila   51
Anderson, Donna   121
Andress, Ursula   140,154,167
Astaire, Fred   19

B

Bacall, Lauren   42,43,57,105
Balitran, Celine   295
Ball, Anne   149
Bardot, Brigitte   92,93,118,142
Bathiat, Arlette   35
Bazlen, Brigid   126
Beatty, Warren 136,148,206,246
Bening, Annette   246
Bergman, Ingrid   97,98,99
Berry, Halle   3,262,300,301
Birkin, Jane   172
Blackman, Honor   128,129
Bogarde, Dirk   138
Bogart, Humphrey   42,43,57
Bon Jovi, Jon   275
Borgnine, Ernest   101
Branagh, Kenneth   232,233
Brando, Marlon   68,146
Bronson, Charles   126
Brooks, Mel   207
Brosnan, Cassandra   225
Brosnan, Pierce
       3,214,225,278,279,300
Brynner, Doris   126,127
Brynner, Yul   126,127,159

Burton, Richard
       56,70,78,94,143,184

C

Cagney, James   113
Caine, Michael   139,152,153,193
Cannon, Dyan   183
Chaplin, Charlie   10/11,17
Cherry, Helen   57
Christie, Julie   145,172,197
Cilento, Diane   180
Clooney, George   286,295,305
Coburn, James   181,207,241
Colbert, Claudette   21,40
Collins, Joan   203
Connors, Michael   150
Connery, Sean
       128,129,141,146,180
Cooper, Gary   30,87
Costner, Kevin   236,237
Courtauld-Thomson, Lord   28
Crawford, Gabrielle   172
Cribbins, Bernard   173
Crowe, Russell   299
Cruise, Tom
   240,248,249,270,280, 281,310
Cummins, Peggy   57
Curtis, Tony   101,105,149

D

Damon, Matt   298
Davenport, Jack   298
Davis, Bette   20,104

Day, Doris   83
De Niro, Robert   190,272
Dean, James   79
Dench, Judi   102,168,237
Deneuve, Catherine   147
Depardieu, Gérard   245,252
Depp, Johnny
       263,267,273,285,306
DiCaprio Leonardo   308
Dietrich, Marlene   68
Douglas, Kirk   58,105,111
Douglas, Michael
       192,208,209,295
Duvall, Robert   204,219,244

E

Eastwood, Clint   162,163,176
Ekland, Britt   122,188
Ercy, Elizabeth   152

F

Fairbanks Jnr, Douglas   55,86
Farr, Felicia   135
Field, Shirley Anne   131
Fields, Gracie   14,23
Fields, W C   18
Flavin, Jennifer   257
Fletcher, Louise   194
Flynn, Errol   112,118
Fonda, Henry   112,187
Fonda, Jane   137,155,182
Fontaine, Joan   32,38,48
Ford, Glenn   122
Ford, Harrison   268

Foster, Barry   173
Foster, Jodie   196,238
Freeman, Morgan   302/303

G

Gable, Clark   16,48,117
Gabor, Zsa Zsa   49,75
Garbo, Greta   9,12,13
Gardner, Ava   62,64,70,71,84
Garland, Judy   138
Garson, Greer   69
Gates, Phyllis   116
George, Susan   179
Gere, Richard   234
Gibson, Mel   215,261,274
Gottsegen, Lisa   212
Grable, Betty   22,168
Granger, Stewart   84
Grant, Cary   96,98,99
Grant, Hugh   276,277,293
Greco, Cosetta   51
Greenwood, Joan   57
Guinness, Alec   114

H

Hanks, Tom   271
De Havilland, Olivia   25,65,115
Helpmann, Robert   54
Hepburn, Katharine
       8,45,54,72,77,170
Hepburn, Audrey
       45,63,73,81,130,310
Heston, Charlton   114
Hitchcock, Alfred   146,173

Hobbs, Lyndall 200
Hobson, Valerie 114
Hoffman, Dustin
178,179,212,213
Holden, William 108,109
Hope, Bob 20,26,27,50
Hopkins, 214,220/221,
   Anthony 233,255,271
Howard, Trevor 37,57,207
Hudson, Rock 116,185
Hurley, Elizabeth 276,293

J

Jackson, Glenda 193
Jackson, Samuel L 304
Jolie, Angelina 296,297

K

Kaye, Danny 38
Keaton, Buster 44
Keaton, Diane 210,288
Keaton, Eleanor 44
Kelly, Gene 31,85,121,183
Kelly, Grace 124,125,171
Kendall, Suzy 160
Kidman, Nicole 240,248,249

L

Ladd, Alan 6/7,52,53,59
Lake, Veronica 24
Law, Jude 298
Leigh, Janet 41,80,84
Leigh, Vivien 35,67,88
Lemmon, Jack 134,135,210,223
Lockwood, Margaret 20
Lollobrigida, Gina
51,66,106,107117
Lombard, Carole 16
Loren, Sophia 68,74,95,123,184

M

Martin, Dean 176
Marvin, Lee 157,186
McGregor, Ewan 307
McKellen, Sir Ian 251
McMillan, Isabell 150
McQueen, Steve 126,131,169
Milland, Ray 28,156
Miller, Arthur 90,91
Mills, John 15,28
Minnelli, Liza 183
Mitchell, Mrs Stephen 75
Mitchell, Yvonne 114
Monroe, Marilyn 90,91
Moore, Demi 227,266,267,275
Moore, Roger 134,151,188,193
More, Kenneth 75
Moss, Kate 273,285
Murad, Paula 241

N

Newman, Paul 110,130,191
Nicholson, Jack
2,194/195,200,201
Niven, David 31,33,75,84

O

Oberon, Merle 40
Olivier, Laurence 22,91
O'Toole, Peter 132,133

P

Pacino, Al 174/175
Paltrow, Gwyneth 284,289,298
Paradis, Vanessa 306
Peck, Gregory 6/7,59,60,61
Penn, Sean 226,242,243
Peters, Jon 189
Pike, Rosamund 300

Pitt, Brad 284,292
Pitts, ZaSu 18
Poitier, Sidney 160,181
Potter, Phyllis 19
Prentiss, Paula 126

R

Reade, Dolores 26
Redford, Robert 150,202
Redgrave, Vanessa 144,177
Reed, Oliver 165
Reeve Christopher
204,205,264,265
Reeve, Dana 265
Reynolds, Burt 183,254,255
Ritchard, Cyril 54
Roberts, Julia 239,250,311
Robinson, Edward G 119,171
Rogers, Ginger 19
Rosin, Sheyla 159
Russell, Jane 1,34,76
Russell, Major E T 53
Ryan, Meg 235

S

Schwarzenegger, Arnold
164,216,217, 256,258/259,295
Scott, Janette 114
Sellers, Peter 122
Shimkus, Joanna 181
Shriver, Marie 295
Sinatra, Frank 39,64,105
Smith, Will 294
Spacey, Kevin 287
Stallone, Sylvester
211,222,257,258/259,260,261
Steiger, Rod 89,186
Stewart, James 82,83,161
Streep, Meryl 199,224
Streisand, Barbra 158,159,189

Swanson, Gloria 36

T

Taylor, Elizabeth
29,37,46,47,143
Taylor, Robert 37
Temple, Shirley 150,166
Tersmeden, Hjordis 31
Tetzel, Joan 6/7,59
Thomas, Henry 292
Thurman, Uma 309
Tracy, Spencer 54,170
Travolta, John 198
Turner, Kathleen 218,251
Turner, Lana 32,103

W

Wagner, Robert 131
Walker, Zena 78
Washington, Denzel
229,230,231,253
Wayne, John 100,120
Weaver, Sigourney 215,269,288
Welch, Raquel 167,176
Wilde, Colette 86
Williams, Cara 113
Willis, Bruce
227,258/259,261,266,267,275
Winslet, Kate 282,283,296
Woodward, Joanne 110,130

Z

Zeta-Jones, Catherine
246,247,290,291,295

Picture Credits
Photographs © Associated Newspapers Archive
(additional photographs by Getty Images)

Acknowledgements

The photographs in this book are from the archives of the *Daily Mail*.
Particular thanks to Steve Torrington, Dave Sheppard,
Brian Jackson, Alan Pinnock, Katie Lee, Richard Jones and all the staff.

Thanks also to
Peter Wright, Trevor Bunting, Alison Gauntlett,
Melanie Cox, Kate Santon, Cliff Salter and John Dunne.